Publishe

Intelek Inte

For: Georgina
Norwich
Dec. 6ᵗʰ 2016

ISBN 978-0-9564637-1-5

Cover design: Intelek International, Norfolk, UK
Typesetting: Intelek International, Norfolk, UK
                     Innovative Design Studio (Barbados)

Acknowledgements

A number of people have assisted me in bringing this book to its present state.

Particularly, I wish to thank Professor Hillary Beckles of the University of the West Indies. His enthusiasm upon reading a preliminary draft of this text was very encouraging.

So too were the overall remarks of Edward Cumberbatch, former General Secretary of the Caribbean Conference of Churches.

I must also express my appreciation to Canon Noel Titus, Principal of Codrington College. I had sought his opinion on some of the substantive issues raised here from as far back as September 1992. I have sought as far as possible within my own vision for this text, to heed his counsel.

Thanks also to Dr. John Holder, also of Codrington College for his constructive observations.

Special thanks must also be extended to my friend David Harvey, a kindred spirit whose initial support for this work was immeasurable.

Special thanks too to friends Andrew and Ashley Skeete for helping me put bread on my table (and letting me eat at theirs) when my finances suffered as a result of my commitment to this book. To fellow writers Margaret Gill and Esther Phillips who though not in agreement with every detail of this undertaking were nonetheless supportive of my effort.

Last but by no means least, I must say thanks to all those who responded to the limited pre-publishing promotion that I did for this book. The eager interest you expressed in reading the published product has helped me to reach this stage. I trust that this book will challenge and be a blessing to you.

Dedication

For my late father, Geoffrey Campbell and my mother
Lucille Campbell,
whose image I bear as much in my mind
as everywhere else in me.
You are the history that touches and teaches me most.

For my brother Wayne, the same but different;
at one, at odds: always loved.

For Ava, Susan, Yvette, Cheryl, Jamal, Dwayne,
Jeremy and Renia.
My closest family

Note: The preceding dedication was written in the mid to late 1990s. In 2002 I became a husband and in 2005 a father, for the first time. In 2009 my daughter Lily was blessed with a brother, Luca, and Sharon and I with a son. I share with Sharon, Lily and Luca a bond of being that defies expression.

I am both pleased and obliged to mention them on this page. Theirs are the presents and futures that most intimately impact who I am.

Author's Foreword

The publication of this book has been a long time coming. I first advertised its "impending" publication in the Nation, a Barbadian newspaper, on July 30th, 1993.

On their own, the reasons behind the delays and deferrals of this book's publication could make another document of similar length. Indeed, I am currently documenting some of those reasons in another literary project entitled "Playing through the Line". Among other things, that collection of my writings – poetry, prose, musical lyrics, diary entries and memos... *graphe* aesthetic and utilitarian - offers readers insights into the minefield of Barbados' academic politics, a tributary of the conservative, elitist elements Barbados' educational system has inherited from its British colonizers.

I believe that while my own concerns about the possible disruptive social impact of this book had a retarding effect on its publication, cultural forces of elitism and opportunism present in the island - and some based here in the UK and in the USA - also conspired against my efforts.

With the benefit of hindsight, spanning some sixteen years, it has become clear to me that even some of those elites who were among this book's most enthusiastic supporters originally, have over time come to question either the usefulness of this text as a catalyst for positive social change, or the benefit of having that change associated with me - arguably a virtual social and political non-entity in my beloved country.

Over time I have come to think that while my recognition of the ramifications of what I set out to achieve with this book was at times overwhelming, my failure to publish it myself until now is at least equally a result of the machinations of Barbadian clerics, academics, business persons, politicians and their satellites. I have come to the conclusion that driven by a variety of motivations, ranging from expedience to envy, and what one lecturer at the University of the West Indies called "academic greed ", some Barbadians who might have assisted me in getting this book published not only chose not to do so, but ultimately sought to prevent its publication.

This intellectual espionage seems all the more plausible if, as I suspect, some individuals in Barbados, the UK and the US have already set about representing ideas they first encountered in an earlier draft of this text as their own.

Actually, one prominent Barbadian academic has told me quite frankly that he wished he had written the book.

I applaud him for his honesty. I doubt though that the enthusiasm he has expressed for the credit that might be associated with the writing of this text would be matched with a willingness to embrace the blame, slander, belittling and other suffering it has caused me.

It has not been easy being the author of a book that, as I see it, may have rocked the foundations of Christianity, or as I say in the poem below, "bombed the Vatican".

The Book

This is the book that bombed the Vatican
This is the book that won the concession;
That brought Pope Paul to his knees;
And to think that all I wanted was peace.

This is the book that grieves and glorifies
The book that speaks the truth and lies.
This is our seed;

The body of our greed,
the corpus and the creed of sacred carnage,
every letter, word and sentence,
every comma, every image,
alive,
dead;
this is the deed dread
dripping red, effervescent;

7

the epiphany ever present.

This is the elixir,
the alchemical fixer of the mind:
the captive conviction and the fine
on those who believe
the tension between the lines that deceive;
and there's no reprieve, for the smoker,
no ease for the joker who overstates this seriousness;
the burning Bush may blight or bless
blind or remind your eye
of what you have seen
verisimilitude,
verily, a dream;

Powering the peoples across the conti nets
rolling the di on our waters,
lest we wake and forget
what we mean;
what wetness is worth
labor's birth
poetic work
justice's dream.

These stanzas hint at some of the deep personal conflict and social
dislocation this book has caused me.

For one thing, the fact that the text has up to now remained
officially "unpublished", though copies of the manuscript have
received substantial circulation, has meant that my voice has to some
degree been silenced, while "my ideas" are to varying degrees being
subjected to public discussion: in essence, it could be said that I have
been alienated from the proceeds - especially social processes -
created or catalyzed by my intellectual labors.

I do not think there is another pain in human experience that can be
compared with the anguish of such profoundly grievous violation of

8

one's personhood. A victim of rape may possibly furnish the closest comparison.

Particularly painful, has been the pain and frustration of isolation, as several of my efforts to engage constructively about religious and other issues with members of Barbadian, British and other societies have been blocked or undermined by persons who apparently feel threatened by me or, for some reason, "uncertain" of my intentions.

Still, today, as I re-read what I wrote here so many years ago, my overwhelming feeling is not one of blaming, bitterness or an inclination to seek revenge: it is a sense of accomplishment. I am profoundly pleased.

I am pleased that I was able to formulate and *articulate* the ideas expressed here, even though I may not have been able until now to publicly and formally represent them as my own to as broad an audience as possible.

It is one thing to apply ideas and principles outlined or inferred in this book in discussions on radio call-in programs and other public fora - as I have been doing in Barbados for many years and continue to do since moving to England.

It is quite another thing, however, to produce the text in which I had documented those ideas and principles. The circumstances being what they have been for me, the sense of satisfaction, accomplishment and even *security*, is immeasurable.

Despite the determined efforts of professorial pretenders, puppet pressmen and plagiaristic priests, I have managed to preserve my legacy. I have preserved my contribution to the shaping of history, in Barbados and beyond. In this book, and through its publication, it is I - not they - who tell *my* story.

This is not a flawless text, neither in form nor content. The inclusion of extensive, personal and organizational detail at the back of the book, before the index – an index that itself contains some unconventional elements – may seem out of place to some readers.

However, I believe the information shared supplies vital support to the overall objectives of the text. Its inclusion is consistent with the goal of *activism* that is central to my own and the book's primary purpose. As a colleague at my former employers City College Norwich commented, on perusing a preliminary draft, this book

9

certainly has *academic* characteristics. It is however, far from a purely academic work.

This is not to suggest that the book offers unassailable arguments. I see where, for example, I am perhaps at risk of being accused of the same fundamentalist treatment of scripture that I am challenging, as one senior Anglican cleric (possibly Dr. John Holder, now the Anglican Bishop of Barbados) observed several years ago.

Yet this does not alter the book's fundamental points. Indeed, as I observe world events today, my original belief that this book can advance "the Kingdom of God" is being radically reinforced, and I am struck by the *timeliness* of it now, notwithstanding its rather belated release.

As Barbados and Britain, like many other predominantly Christian countries around the world come to grips with the worldwide threat of Islamic-fundamentalist inspired terrorism, this book offers an arguably compelling, albeit perhaps unexpected solution. It suggests that rather than a reactionary digging of our heels deeper into seemingly safe, immoveable, orthodox faith positions, Christianity's most fruitful and helpful response to the "Muslim Question", resides in a radical rethinking of our own religion.

It suggests that this "rethinking", or *reformation* – which, arguably, has up to now been merely a feature of elitist, marginal, contested and even "disreputable" segments of the collective body Christian - be now brought into a central discourse where it may more coherently and consistently challenge conventional notions.

The need for precisely such a *foregrounding* of this "rethinking" was demonstrated in 2008 when the Archbishop of Canterbury, Dr. Rowan Williams was pilloried by other Anglicans, the British press and members of the general public for suggesting that UK legislators may one day want to consider incorporating or accommodating some aspects of Islamic Sharia law in Britain's legal system.

While deficiencies in the media's coverage of what the Archbishop actually said may be largely to blame for the public's overreaction (and a general antagonism between the media and religious institutions is an abiding concern of mine), I find it hard to resist the view that primary responsibility for the debacle that ensued must be placed firmly at the feet of Christians.

To elaborate, I believe that Christians' complacency and self-satisfaction with the level of teaching that obtains in the average, mainstream pubic sermon - amounting to an uncritical affirmation of conventional Christian traditions - was the overarching factor that led to the public's apprehension over what the Archbishop said.

The fact is, average British Christians - like their Barbadian counterparts - simply are not used to having their religious world views so authoritatively and directly challenged or impinged on by their own leaders.

This is true notwithstanding the Church of England's decades long controversial engagement with the issue of homosexuality and in particular, gay marriage.

In his foreword below, written at least ten years ago, Barbadian cleric Reverend Andrew Hatch (now retired) cites the failure of himself and other priests to engage difficult questions pertaining to the faith of the Christian flocks they served. I am certain he once told me that the essential problem was a failure of energy among the clerics. I have long wondered if it may be a species of laziness, perhaps inspired by Christians' complacency with their privileged status in Barbados (as in the UK, USA and elsewhere) as the national religion.

Fundamentally, "The Bible: Beauty and Terror Reconciled" challenges Christian complacency, however derived. It challenges all Christians - priests and *pewpeople* - of whatever denomination, to extend their understanding of the "mystery of Godliness" beyond the constraints of their current comfort zone.

It challenges all of us to set aside denominational, cultural and national interests, if only for the purpose of this reading exercise, and contemplate the teachings of the Bible from a truly personal, authentic conscience oriented perspective.

Clearly, a failure of conscience is at the root of the long-running pedophile scandal that has besieged Roman Catholicism. What is perhaps not so clear, is the failure of conscience in Western theological reflection that is reducing the average Sunday sermon to a kind of pedagogical pedophilia.

Junior Campbell
July 2010

Foreword by Trevor Marshall
Historian, Barbados Community College

It is a distinct pleasure and an honour to offer a foreword to this new work by Junior Campbell, a young author of extremely positive promise. My attention was first drawn to Campbell's work when he published his first work - a humorous look at Barbadian cultural traits.

In this new work Campbell, a very spiritual individual who searches for righteousness as against religiosity, explores the theme of man's relationship to his maker, with his fellow man and with his own humanity.

Campbell has described himself as a freethinker and it is because of his search for the quintessence of spirituality that he has written this book. In it he subjects all of the received tenets of Christian spiritualism to acute examination. He looks at the received wisdom of the Bible with fresh eyes and mature vision, exploring the hidden meanings in its pages and attempting to distil for himself the pearls of wisdom which bible scholars and secular searchers after wisdom have inwardly digested.

It is unusual for one so young and for someone outside the cloistered walls of a religious seminary to delve so deeply into the mystery of our presence on this earth, but I must note that Campbell is now at that age at which the historical Jesus Christ himself consummated his earthly ministry and that makes this exploratory work all the more compelling in its significance.

For me Campbell's small volume is extremely significant, both in what he says and in its timing. This volume comes at a time in the life of our nation when standards of morality and discipline appear to have declined considerably and there is a dearth of serious thoughts emanating from thinkers on our moral and spiritual condition. Campbell's book goes a long way towards filling that need and it provides us with a considerable number of thought provoking ideas. This book will inspire and encourage all readers with its challenging notions and its direct, forthright style of writing.

I consider it a significant publication in a large number of respects and wish to place on record my appreciation to the writer for the way in which he has handled such a challenging topic.

Foreword by Canon Andrew Hatch
Anglican diocese of Barbados

A technician at Barbados Rediffusion where, twice weekly, I moderate Down To Brass Tacks said to me: 'Father Hatch, you obviously have inside knowledge of the Bible that the rest of us do not. 'On the contrary', I replied, 'the explanations I offer questioners on the Bible represent a critical approach that has been accepted in the mainstream churches for a hundred years. The pity is that priests and ministers have not troubled to share these insights with the faithful.'

Let us not use the word 'myth' for many OT stories for fear of being wilfully misunderstood, but as in the New Testament, for every precious teaching, the Old Testament employs 'parables'. The two creation stories in Gen 1-2:4a and Gen 2: 4b-25 are such parables. They convey religious not historical truth. But truths they do convey:

- that divine purpose lies behind creation
- God made everything good
- the world did not come into existence by chance or by itself
- the process was designed to lead up to the making of man in the divine image.

One further elementary point: revelation is progressive. We advance from Ps 137.9 'Blessed shall he be that taketh thy children and dasheth them against the rocks.' to Mk 10:14 'Suffer the little children to come unto me and forbid them not.'

Bishop Spong of Newark wrote a book 'Rescuing the bible from fundamentalists': Junior Campbell's "The Bible - beauty and terror reconciled" is an excellent Caribbean approach to the same menace that keeps so many good people enslaved to an Old Testament God. It will facilitate discussion and critical thinking and should lead to a greater tolerance. I experience on Brass Tacks, the wrath - not to call it venom - of fundamentalists who short-change our God accepting that He gives faith but forgetting that he is also the creator of our brain.

Overview of Chapters

Introduction: Background and basic thrust.

The introduction gives details on the author's experience and the general direction of the text. Specific problems arising from the fundamentalist treatment of scripture are cited. Aspects of the fundamentalist psyche are highlighted.

Specific mention is made of the vulnerability of Caribbean and other third world societies to fundamentalism. Finally, the proposed reformed concept of the New Covenant (conscience) is introduced.

Chap. 1 The nature and scope of the problem.

Here the origin and extent of the problem is briefly examined. Denominational groups associated with the problem are identified by name. A more detailed statement of the books approach and objectives is made: the literary-historical approach recommended by traditional mainstream churches and adopted by the author is introduced.

Chap. 2 Examining the fundamentalist doctrine of inerrancy and infallibility.

The purported scriptural basis of this doctrine is examined and shown to be lacking in several ways. Following theologian James Barr ("Escaping From Fundamentalism", 1984, SCM Press Ltd, London), an interpretation of the same passages of the Bible that is in line with mainstream churches' (Anglican, Roman Catholic and so on) emphasis on *tradition* is offered as a possible alternative reading.

Chap. 3 The true basis of fundamentalism.

This chapter is divided into four subsections, each of which is named after and highlights a historical factor deemed to be at the root of the fundamentalist problem. The subsections are: i) The influence of legalistic Judaism. ii) The introduction and establishment of the ekklesia in Christianity. iii) The creation of a distinctly Christian canon. and iv) The error of the Reformers.

Chap. 4   The New Covenant: a human phenomenon?

Here the concept of the New Covenant is more fully explored and shown to be a universal, human phenomenon - not exclusive to Christianity. Its identification by other names and operation in other faiths is noted. Specifically, the operation of this phenomenon in the Brahmin priesthood is highlighted. The identification of this phenomenon as the Logos and conscience is also discussed. Preparation is made for the author's subsequent focus on conscience as the author proposes that appreciating the beauty of the Bible and overcoming the "terror" of it means learning to understand and trust our consciences.

Ch. 5   Conscience vindicated

First, the academic and empirical basis of the author's understanding of conscience are put in perspective. Conscience is discussed both from the perspective of secular authorities and biblical evidence. The ambiguity of conscience is treated as an inevitable, inescapable and instructive reality. The acknowledgement of conscience as the "final" authority - notwithstanding it's ambiguity - is urged. The point is made that the ambiguity of conscience should serve to stimulate grace, i.e. tolerance.

Further attention is given to the simplistic, perfectionist mindset of fundamentalism and the dangers associated with it. Fundamentalism's artificial divorcing of the natural and the supernatural is treated. It is suggested that conscience be seen as a divine-human dialogue. This idea is elaborated in the final chapter.

Ch. 6   Respecting God's word - limits included.

This chapter focuses on the limits of our knowledge, especially our knowledge of the answers to the 'deeper questions' of life - questions about God etc.

The inexhaustibility of these questions and the importance of affirming people rather than convictions is emphasized. A landmark experience behind the author's arrival at this conclusion is recounted. The text closes on a humility engendering, compassionate and conciliatory note.

About this book

This book presents my basic opinions about the Bible. Among other things, these opinions have been inspired by my experience of the Bible in a Barbadian fundamentalist Christian context.

I was a member of the People's Cathedral, led by Reverend Holmes Williams for approximately eight years (1982 - 1990/91). I also fellowshipped freely with a wide cross-section of other Evangelical Christians, holding what I would call *ex officio* membership in at least two other churches: Love Gospel Assembly, led by Pastor Noel Goddard and Revival Time Assembly, led by Pastor David Durant.

It was among the fundamentalists that I learnt to take the Bible literally - an approach that can be beneficial (it would not be so popular if that was not true) but is also fraught with very real dangers.

My views on the Bible have also been influenced by mainstream Christianity. I have had, and still have, significant dialogue with leaders and members of mainstream churches - particularly Anglicans (called Episcopalian in the USA), Roman Catholics and the marginally mainstream Methodists.

One of the key issues dealt with here is the contradictory role of mainstream Christianity in preaching reconciliation (or as one Anglican cleric put it, "generosity of spirit") but still perpetuating the division breeding, fundamentalist perception of the scriptures that I call the "terror of the Bible".

At the very least, my views on this matter should prove useful for persons who want to understand some of the factors and dynamics behind the current emphasis on evangelism by mainstream church leaders, especially Anglicans and Catholics.

I would also take this opportunity to inform readers that I dialogue frequently with members of the Rastafarian faith, a movement which, because of its emphasis on individualism on the one hand and literalistic use of the Bible to "legislate" public morality on the other, provides an excellent opportunity for observing the conflict between these two phenomena.

Rastafarianism has influenced my understanding of the Bible in a rather interesting and paradoxical way. During my fundamentalist Christian days, I regarded Rastas as total heretics and marijuana

17

peddling outlaws. In fact, I was totally surprised some years ago (1996) when one member of the local Rastafarian community told me that they consider themselves Christians.

It suddenly dawned on me that some of these dreadlocked people actually believe they are serving the same God that Christians claim to serve; the God of the Bible. I realized that Rastas actually have a similar opinion of the Bible as fundamentalist Christians.

That was quite a revelation for me. I think it demonstrates how ignorance, prejudice and popular (including media) propaganda can prevent one from realizing how much one has in common with others who may, speak, dress or otherwise appear different from oneself.

I am not suggesting that I now agree with everything Rastafarians believe in. I still have some difficulty with the complicated Marijuana issue - the health and legal aspects of the issue particularly.

However, I remain personally committed to dialogue and co-operation with persons in this movement, and to promoting dialogue between Rastafarians and other Christians or Christian-minded persons..

In addition to casual, at times heated, but mostly cordial exchanges with Rastafarian members of the general public, I have had significant interaction with such influential Rastafarians as Sociologist Dr. Ikal Tafari, now deceased, and Ras Iral Jabari Talma of Barbados; also, Rastafarian attorney and politician Miguel Lorne and singer Luciano (Jepther McClymott) of Jamaica and Nasio Fontaine, formerly of Dominica, now resident in the U.S.A.

I also include exchanges with Ibo Cowper, formerly of the Jamaican band Third World, and well known Rastafarian "authority" Baptist Reverend Clinton Chisholm among my sources of insight into Rastafarian thought.

As far as written sources are concerned, I am mainly dependent on Howard Campbell's Rasta and Resistance.

As with the thoughts shared regarding the Rastafarian movement in this book, my interaction with Rastafarians generally has been guided by both my sense of identity with them, as an Afro-Caribbean person, and a concern for them, as a former fundamentalist Christian myself. I see worrying similarities between some Rastafarians' approach to Bible reading and interpretation and that of fundamentalist Christians.

18

I shared some of these concerns with Rastafarians from around the region during an "extra-sessional" gathering of the 1997 Caribbean Rastafarian Mini-summit at the Clement Payne Cultural Centre in Barbados.

Last, but by no means least, my views on the Bible have been shaped by my own persistent study of the Bible, church history and religious history in general. It is this determination to acquire what I call in one essay an *Informed Faith* - a faith based on intelligent inquiry, honest self-knowledge and corresponding selectivity, that is, personal choice - that has shaped my opinion of the Bible.

I have mixed feelings about the Bible, some positive, some negative. This book demonstrates how I have reconciled those feelings - how I have come to terms with both the beauty and terror of the Bible.

This book is therefore likely to offend persons who embrace fundamentalist Christianity's literalistic, idealistic perception of the Bible uncritically. Persons who believe that Christian fundamentalism is the unquestionable will of God for them will have difficulty seeing any benefit in this book. I do not hold that against them. I once shared the same kind of religious outlook.

This book will be valued more highly by those who have doubts about fundamentalism; those who sense and want to come to terms with its dangers. I have met a lot of people like that since I started to publicize this book.

This book offers assistance to persons who find fundamentalist Christian doctrine and practice questionable and want to learn about less literalistic and, alternately, more holistic or comprehensive ways of understanding the Bible.

I believe some things in the Bible should be taken literally. For example, the reader will find that I take the biblical description of the "New Covenant" as a spiritual phenomenon very literally. I therefore feel very strongly about fundamentalist churches' (evangelical and mainstream) tendency to confuse the spiritual phenomenon called the New Covenant, with the material, literal phenomenon that is the New Testament - the biblical books from Matthew to Revelation.

My understanding of the nature and purpose of the New Covenant stems from an essentially literal, "plain reading" rendering of biblical passages on this subject – passages like Jeremiah 31:31-34.

However, this understanding, being holistic, extends beyond what is written in those passages and draws on the extra-biblical history of Judaism and Christianity; on the history of other religions and on theories of social and psychological dynamics which are supported by the Bible and other literary sources.

In other words, I have found that a literal, or what fundamentalists call a "plain meaning" approach to biblical passages on the New Covenant, also obliges, or at least inclines one, to look at these same passages from a larger historical, social and psychological perspective.

Some people may add an economic perspective as a separate angle but I subsume economic issues under the social heading. This should not be taken as an indication that I underestimate the significance of these issues though. My treatment of the issue of priestcraft here should make it clear that I do not.

So, you can say that I still take the Bible literally, but that is only a point of departure for me. I have found that a truly sound appreciation of this ancient text requires a more holistic or comprehensive approach.

If you already share that opinion, or are inclined to, you will find this book helpful.

Title changes

I started writing this book around 1984. At that time, I was a young evangelical, Pentecostal Christian, zealous to do the will of God. I wanted to use every waking moment of every day for Jesus.

Then, as now, I felt that this was, or should be the natural desire of every Christian. So I started to write a book called, "What On Earth Are You Doing?!"

That title captured the sense of impatience, and annoyance I was feeling as I watched many of my fellow Christians go from day to day "wasting time" - as I saw it.

You see, back then I believed that this earth is just a "transit point" for humanity. This belief is still held by most Barbadian Pentecostals I suspect, but many evangelicals, including the influential Bahamian preacher Miles Munroe and a number of his Barbadian "Kingdom NOW" preaching associates have apparently changed their minds on this question.

Anyway, back in those days I was persuaded that I was going to heaven, sooner or later, so I had to make the most of my time on earth.

Through the "What On Earth Are You Doing?!" project, I was urging myself and other Christians to get busy, "redeeming the time, because the days are evil", as the Bible puts it (Ephesians 5:16, King James Version).

It was at this time of consolidation - the time of my first really serious efforts to order my worldly affairs in a manner that would help me make the most of my time, knowledge, energy, money, and so on - that I started to really delve deeply into the Bible.

I had been taught that God's perfect will was contained in this perfect, inerrant and infallible book, and I believed that.

I was totally unprepared for what I found: questions, questions and more questions.

Questions about the authorship of the Four Gospels: it turned out that these were originally anonymous documents.

Questions about the apocryphal books of the Old and the New Testament: some apocryphal Old Testament books are quoted and or alluded to in parts of the New Testament. The reference to someone

21

being "sawn asunder" in Hebrews 11:37 is an example.

Even questions about the correct English translation of the name of the Christian savior. For some reason (probably political reasons related to anti-Jewish sentiment among British Christians in those days) the King James Translators rejected the "plain meaning" English translation "Joshua", choosing the exceptional "Jesus" - a transliteration of the Greek *Iesous*, achieved by changing the "I" to a "J" and taking out the "O".

Now, such questionable or anomalous matters are not a big thing if you have been taught to expect and make allowances for such shortcomings in the pages of scripture.

However, if like I and other fundamentalists you were told that you could, indeed must trust the Bible because it is accurate and reliable in every "itsy-bitsy" historical, geographical, cosmological detail - every "jot and tittle" - if that is what you were led to believe, well then, such biblical anomalies can be really disturbing!

If like I, and many other fundamentalists Christians, you had been induced to regularly part with ten percent of your income because the Bible says "You rob me by not giving a tithe of your income to the church" (a rough paraphrase of Malachi 3:8; a passage of scripture of which some preachers are particularly fond), biblical obscurity about the compulsory nature of tithing can really upset you!

So, being a Bible trusting, tithe paying Pentecostal fundamentalist, the discovery of numerous biblical anomalies and questions really upset me.

More on that later though. My point here, is that the anger and confusion I felt led me to start "another" book; this book, which I initially called "The Terror Of The Bible".

It is really just one book though. It has taken me approximately thirteen years of considerable soul searching and personal healing to come to the place where I can clearly see and say that the two books are inseparable.

From "The Terror Of The Bible", I changed the title to "Overcoming the Terror Of The Bible", to highlight the positive, constructive aspects of the book.

Then, in an effort to make the title more positive still, I added a subtitle, making it "Overcoming the Terror of the Bible - Appreciating Its Worth".

This was a major development, signaling a personal victory. I was indeed healing. I was coming to the place where I was more willing to admit that there could not only be value - but beauty, in the Bible.

I was developing a greater level of tolerance for those who only see the Bible's beauty. I was proposing an accommodation with those willfully or otherwise blind to its shortcomings.

Along with this growth in tolerance came the title "The Bible: beauty or terror?" which signaled a greater willingness on my part to let everyone decide for themselves what the Bible means to them.

Next came the title "The Bible: Truth or Terror" but I was not entirely comfortable with that title because I felt that the term "truth" may evoke a literalism that I do not mean to communicate.

My understanding of "truth" is holistic - I try to see the whole picture - or at least as much of it as can be seen. The "truth" of the Bible to which I will be drawing readers' attention is not the simplistic "truth" of literalistic, shallow, superficial fundamentalism.

So, I decided to go back to the earlier title "The Bible: Beauty or Terror"! I made that decision after a conversation with award winning Barbadian poet and feminist activist Margaret Gill, in which she quoted the poet John Keats cryptic equation '"Beauty is truth, truth beauty," – that is all ye know on earth and all ye need to know.' During that conversation we also talked about the relationship between "symmetry" and "beauty".

Symmetry has been defined as "beauty resulting from balanced or harmonious arrangement". This is what I have been trying to achieve in the form and content of this book, and also through its publication.

On the 19th of October 1997 I decided, to make what would be the final modification to the title of this book. That is when I decided I will call it, The Bible: Beauty and Terror Reconciled.

A word about words

We need to be careful with words. Words can be easily misunderstood and misused.

Words serve important functions such as expressing, clarifying, communicating and "storing" information and ideas. However, words - especially written words - also have a way of being confused with, obscuring and otherwise obstructing or negating the very information and ideas they were originally intended to express, clarify, communicate, store etc.

One of the things that has made the writing and publishing of "The Bible: beauty and terror reconciled" particularly challenging, is my acute awareness of the complexity, limitations and even potential lethalness of written words.

There were times when I felt like giving up on this book altogether, because I realize that what I am writing here is susceptible to the very same kind of misunderstanding, manipulation and misinterpretation of words that this book is intended to counter and discourage: the kind of misinterpretation and abuse of words that occurs in the case of the Bible.

I am concerned that some interpreters may use the words of this book to promote religious confusion, prejudice, intolerance and divisiveness. I am concerned that it may be used to take advantage of and exploit the innocence and/or ignorance of others - the way many preachers and other public figures use the Bible.

Those are not the kinds of things I set out to achieve. That is not why I am publishing this discourse. I wrote this book in an effort to counter those kinds of things; those kinds of "crimes against humanity" that the Bible and other religious texts have been used to perpetrate from time immemorial.

This book is intended to promote tolerance among persons of diverse cultures, faiths and outlooks. My primary aim is to show how "scripture" - whether it is the Jewish, Brahmin, Christian, Islamic or any other "scripture" (Greek *graphe* = [the/these] things written) - may be used to unite people, rather than divide them.

My intention is to show how the Bible can be used to help, bless, edify and bring the fulfillment of self-actualization to all who read it - not just a denominational or ecclesiastical elite.

24

The book Language and Communication by Merlene Cuthbert and Michael Pidgeon (Cedar Press, 1979) makes the very important observation that misunderstandings in communication are more likely between two persons speaking the same language than two persons speaking different languages.

At first glance, this statement seems rather odd, and not likely to be true. However, when you think about it, it makes perfect sense. As Cuthbert explains, misunderstandings between persons speaking the same language are frequent because we assume that people speaking the same language as we do know what we mean, when we say certain words, and we assume that we know what they mean when they speak.

However, within languages they are certain peculiarities (for example, dialects and personal idiosyncrasies) which can make it difficult for two persons speaking the same language to ascertain what each other means to say, whether via spoken or written words.

Surely the reader will be familiar with situations in which a hearer genuinely claims to have "heard" one thing, but the speaker, equally sincerely, claims to have said or meant something else.

The fact is, words can be rather arbitrary, ambiguous and confusing. They can often get in the way of or obstruct the communication of meaning.

Why, even reasonably eloquent speakers are sometimes at a loss for the words to say what they mean. I say this on the authority of first-hand experience.

The confusing nature of words is compounded in the matter of religion where words take on powerful connotations, significant social consequences and peculiarly personal shades of meaning.

Take the Bible, for example. For some people, the Bible can be the most beautiful book in the world. For others, it can be the ugliest, most intimidating, scary, terrorizing document that was ever published.

The distinguishing factor is who is speaking. What is that person's experience of the Bible? Have they read it, or did they just hear about it? How do they read it and interpret it? What school of interpretation do they follow (Catholic, Protestant, Greek Orthodox, Jehovah's Witness, Mormon etc)? What are the factors affecting their reading and interpretation of the Bible?

A person's level or quality of literacy (they may be dyslexic), family background, self-esteem, church affiliation, and even nationality, will affect how they read and interpret the Bible, or any other body of "scripture".

Some people like myself, at times, are naturally more "word-bound" than others and may be in danger of taking scripture too literally. Others may miss important details because they treat words too loosely or take things like the details of church history for granted.

These and other factors shape and determine our ideas and opinions about the Bible. At a fundamental level, they determine whether we focus on and emphasize that which is conciliatory, just, gracious, peace building and beautiful in the Bible, or whether we become pre-occupied with literalism, judging, fear, prejudice and hatred - elements of what I call the terror of the Bible.

The reality of the words of the Bible is largely, though not entirely, a personal, subjective reality. The name "Jesus", words like "church", "sin", "hell", "righteousness" and other common biblical terms tend to mean very little until we personalize them; until we internalize them.

What is more, the subjectivity of words is not only evident from one individual to the next, but can also be demonstrated within the context of a single person's experience.

For example, a person may hear the name "Jesus" a thousand times and it may mean very little to them. They may hear that name one more time, and it may somehow be imbued with vitality, relevance, and life-changing meaning. Some people would call this the moment of truth. Some would call it the moment of saving faith or conviction.

Regardless of what we call it, the question is "What is the difference between that one moment and the other thousand?"

There are possibly a thousand and one answers to that question, and none of them may have anything whatsoever to do with the name "Jesus" itself, at least not directly. The deciding factor(s) would probably have more to do with the particular circumstances or context in which the name was said - where, when, by whom, in relation to what and similar questions.

For example, I have noticed that some Barbadians tend to be more open to church-going, becoming Christians and so on, when they experience unexpected good fortune or blessing. They seem to be more open to the idea that they are obligated to worship God at that time.

One of my goals here is to impress upon the reader the need to first put one's own and then other people's views about the Bible - about "Jesus", "the Church", "sin" "righteousness" and other religious matters - in their correct context.

Why do you believe what you believe about the Bible? Is that what you have always believed? If you have changed your mind, why did you do so?

Some people treat the words of the Bible very loosely, using those words to make sweeping generalizations about reality. In a paradoxical way, those generalizations lead to a restriction of those persons' access to the "big picture" of reality. They become unduly narrow-focused - what we commonly call narrow-minded.

I want to encourage people to try to maintain a sense of the whole picture, or at least as much of it as they possibly can. I want to encourage readers of this book to bear in mind that it is folly to make rigid judgments about other people and matters that we know little or nothing about - other than by way of generalization.

It is very easy to make rash judgments about other people's attempts to implement and live their understanding of the Bible when you know little about how that person reads. Do you read me?

Fortunately, like the meanings of words, the significance and influence of the factors which shape our understanding of the Bible and our attitude towards people who see it differently can be changed. Hopefully, when that happens our own understanding of the Bible will have changed for the better. This is my experience. Some people have called it "back-sliding". I call it growth.

Introduction:
Background and basic direction

This book has been inspired by my experience of fundamentalist Christianity. Immediately I will caution the reader that my use of the term fundamentalist here is rather comprehensive. It does not only cover the well known fundamentalist groups (Baptists, Pentecostals etc.) but also includes segments of churches like the Roman Catholic and Anglican church which are known as mainstream churches, and are not always viewed as holding fundamentalist views.

My use of the term is limited to Christianity though. I deal with the issue of fundamentalism among Muslims, Rastafarians and other religious groups elsewhere.

The reader should also note that I tend to use the term evangelical as a synonym for fundamentalist, but I am aware that not all evangelicals are fundamentalists.

In June 1982, prompted by a profound, but mostly emotional conversion experience, I "accepted Jesus Christ as my personal savior".

I was seventeen years old then, and like most members of our "Christianity" saturated Barbadian society, I had some knowledge of the Bible. Also like many Barbadians - and it seems a significant portion of western society - while I had not made a decisive commitment to the Bible's precepts, I basically regarded it as true, that is, the word of God, in the purest sense imaginable.

Upon my conversion and attachment to a local Pentecostal church my idealization of the Bible intensified considerably. I was encouraged in this by fellow church-members and the leadership of that church. However, as I took the Bible more and more seriously, two things happened.

One of these was that I found it increasingly difficult to reconcile much of what I was seeing in the Bible with the conduct and practices of the evangelical community of which I was a part.

I became particularly concerned about the administrative policy of these churches. Among other things, their leadership structures, how

28

leaders were selected, the participation of the congregation in the leadership process, and not least of all, the management of their finances, that is, their tithes and offerings.

I remember being agitated by the fact that although extensive international studies have shown that personal evangelism, that is one-to-one witnessing, is the most efficient and effective means of "soul-winning" (converting people to Christianity), many of these churches persist with expensive radio and TV ministries.

I wondered why that money could not be spent on charitable programs to assist disadvantaged church members. Why, for example, in the midst of an International Monetary Fund (IMF) restructuring program which led to massive job losses and wage cuts in Barbados, little was being done to help adversely affected church members cope. On the contrary, one pastor determined that his first duty was to warn his congregation of the dangers of "robbing God", by failing to pay their tithes!

I began to feel as though only a few evangelical church-leaders were taking God seriously. I felt as though only a few of my Christian friends and associates really cared about winning souls for Jesus or looking after their needy brethren. I gradually became frustrated with my evangelical peers.

After worshipping in the evangelical community for about five years by then, this frustration led to my withdrawal from that group.

I set out virtually on my own, to pursue the will of God in the ideal of absolute surrender. I purposed to give myself totally to God's service. I resigned my job at a local shoe store, moved away from my parents home - so as not to burden them financially - and embarked on a career of open-air preaching and tract writing. My only support was intense bible-study, prayer and odd jobs - weeding, off-loading containers and other manual, occasional jobs.

It was a humbling, solitary existence. I felt misunderstood by most of my former fundamentalist friends. I felt a lot of bitterness and resentment toward several of them. I had to contend with feelings of anger and feelings of guilt over this anger. I was becoming increasingly confused.

The other thing that happened as I sought to live in greater dependence upon the Bible, as conceived and interpreted by fundamentalists, was that my Bible-studies were having the then surprising effect of whittling away at my faith in the Bible itself.

I would be reading my Bible, particularly the Amplified Version which I find rather informative, and would come across a footnote pointing out, for example, that the last twelve verses of the gospel attributed to Mark were not in the earliest manuscripts!

Or I would be reading one of the bible encyclopedias that I purchased at a local Christian Literature Crusade book shop and come across some information which was equally damaging to the common fundamentalist understanding of the Bible's inspiration and preservation. For example, the articles on the texts and manuscripts of the Old and New Testament, which contain references to the scribal errors, deliberate scribal intervention and doctrinal corrections that are in the surviving Hebrew, Aramaic and Greek texts.

It got to the point where I was afraid to continue any in-depth studying of the Bible at all. You see, as a fundamentalist you are told you could lose your soul, if you question the Bible - the word of God.

So, in my anxiety I abandoned all serious, analytical research into the Bible. I put away the Bible encyclopedias, commentaries and other analytical texts I had been reading.

After a period of about five months, I put all my missionary ambitions on hold, and returned to a regular job. The compromise I made in doing this added to my increasing sense of guilt and backsliding.

Eventually, purged of any sense of self-righteousness or indignation, and actually feeling rather lost, I decided to retrace my steps, and go back to the environment in which I had last felt sure of my salvation. I therefore resumed fellowship at my old church, and sought to be reconciled to my evangelical brethren. Gradually, my uncertainty about my relationship with God faded, and I regained my previous assurance of sins forgiven.

However, and on reflection I would have to say fortunately, for me, I was still able to see the same problems and inconsistencies in the churches, that had led me to withdraw from them and I still found myself questioning the fundamentalist understanding of the nature and purpose of scripture.

This time though, I purposed not to let myself be intimidated by the fear of questioning the Bible that had led me to abandon in-depth Bible research. My willingness to return to my old church and submit myself to the leadership there had satisfied me that I was not just seeking to have my own way - as some persons were suggesting. In essence, it convinced me of the integrity and validity of the questions I was asking.

This was a significant milestone for me: I believe that it was at this point of self-affirmation that I started to overcome the terror of the Bible and move toward a more informed appreciation of it.

No longer questioning my own motives, I was free to pursue a critical analysis of the Bible.

As I did so, I became more and more certain that there was something intrinsically wrong with the fundamentalist understanding of the nature and purpose of the Bible.

And so it happened that as I sought to objectively inform my faith - to deepen and enrich my understanding of the will of God as expressed in the Bible - my faith in the fundamentalist doctrine of the inerrancy and infallibility of the Bible was irreversibly undermined.

I want readers to be clear on this. I have taken the time to recount these basic details of my experience because I want readers to understand that my rejection of Christian fundamentalism here is not the result of a personal vendetta or bitterness toward any group or individual. This is the conclusion that many people jumped to when I told them about this book. They were wrong.

This book is the product of my desire to know and serve the God whom fundamentalists represent as (and I agree) the ultimate author of the Bible. It is the product of my singular determination to embrace nothing less than the truth about God, Jesus, the Bible the church and Christianity - however non-traditional or disquieting that truth may be to the fundamentalist psyche.

It was as I pursued the truth, that it became increasingly clear to me that the fundamentalist community's doctrines and practices were prone to be biased because their understanding of the Bible - particularly their belief that it is inerrant and infallible - is rooted in ignorance and biases.

I fought against the inclination to question the Bible's inerrancy and infallibility at first because I felt that my salvation depended on my acceptance of this doctrine. I tried to tell myself that the irregularities of fundamentalist preaching and practice which I was noticing were just the result of the personal biases and preferences of self-centered fundamentalist church-leaders.

I desperately wanted to avoid questioning the Bible. I wanted to have total confidence in it, but could not.

Eventually, this situation led to a brief conversation with the leader of one of the evangelical assemblies with which I was associated, during which I decided that I was better off away from this group.

This conversation followed that individual's reiteration, from the pulpit, of his belief that church administration should not be based on democratic principles because the Bible does not teach democracy. I find this an astounding conclusion - especially since the very word translated "church" in the Bible (the Greek *ekklesia*) has its origin in the democratic government of classical Greece[1].

This though is just one example of the type of unsound unethical and illogical interpretations fundamentalist preachers are capable of extracting from the Bible. I have chosen not to identify this particular fundamentalist preacher precisely for this reason: the problem I am addressing here is a lot bigger than that individual's anti-democratic biases[2]. (This same individual once alluded to the wider problem himself, saying that the Bible can be used to teach anything - a rather daring admission coming from such a person). The problem I am addressing here is the idealistic perception of the Bible as an unquestionable authority, which, combined with its openness - or better, susceptibility, to virtually any interpretation - makes it a potent instrument of abuse.

My primary concern is not the personal biases of this or that Christian or church leader. I recognize that some subjectivity is inevitable, and more than that, legitimate. My main concern is the idealistic perception of the Bible which is used to cloak the subjectivity of its interpreters - clergy and lay people alike.

Countless other Christians exploit this idealistic perception of the Bible - consciously or unconsciously - to justify several other equally inequitable, unethical and unwholesome church policies and practices.

This intimidating perception of the Bible is also behind the divisive and fragmentary character of fundamentalist biblical interpretation - that use of the Bible which encourages wrangling and divisions among fundamentalist Christians internally, and externally, among fundamentalists and society at large.

Not long ago, one Barbadian sociologist[3] did a study in which reference was made to the deterioration of value-consensus in our local communities. Fundamentalist divisiveness was not cited among the causes of this problem in Barbados, but I am certain it contributes to the lack of social cohesion here because members of these notoriously divisive groups constitute a large and vocal segment of the Barbadian churchgoing community.

What is more, some of these fundamentalists hold prominent positions in the commercial, educational, political and other professional spheres of Barbadian society. Their intolerance of and insensitivity toward each other and toward non-fundamentalists has serious implications for the entire church community and society as a whole. If nothing else, the recent controversy over the introduction of a book other than the Bible as part of a program to teach values education in the schools should have convinced Barbadians of this.

The idealism of fundamentalist dogma and its impact on the youth, who are prone to idealism, is also a major concern. Fundamentalism thrives on idealism, particularly that longing, evident among people of all ages, for an infallible guide. It seems there will always be persons looking for an unquestionable, unchanging authority figure of some kind, on whom they can rely for stability.

The fundamentalist perception of the Bible appeals to this impractical desire. However, history is full of examples where the dictates of the Bible became imperceptibly merged with the personality and dictates of its more charismatic human exponents. The consequences can be disastrous. Remember the Jim Jones and David Koresh tragedies?

These are extreme examples. Generally the fundamentalist "bubble" is burst in less horrific fashion.

The trauma the individual psyche suffers in the less sensational and publicized instances of fundamentalist disillusionment is not to be underestimated though. It is widely known that the mental anguish - anger, bitterness and confusion - that comes with religious disillusionment can be devastating, especially to the young. They are particularly prone to the "post fundamentalist syndrome" of giving up on religion altogether.

This syndrome, Which Professor James Barr alludes to in his book Escaping From Fundamentalism[4], is a by-product of fundamentalism's exclusionist claim that it alone faithfully observes and preserves the authority of the Bible and its corresponding systematic inoculation of its adherents, setting them against other forms of Christianity.

These tactics discourage many young people emerging from fundamentalism from considering alternative forms of Christianity (or of any religion).

I am particularly concerned for young people in places like the Caribbean, Central and South America and Africa who, because of the social and economic pressures that face developing nations, are more vulnerable to the idealistic, escapist appeal of fundamentalism.

A related issue is the serious challenge Fundamentalism poses to education - and consequently to human development - because of its anti-intellectual bias. Serious or essentially objective thinking and Bible analysis is discouraged.

I once questioned a senior pastor about the canonization of scripture, in particular querying who had decided that the Spirit of God had stopped inspiring writers, when and why. I had come to view the Church's canonization of scripture - the designation of only certain books as divinely inspired - as an essentially arbitrary process.

The pastor, who was either unable or unwilling to answer these questions, became very irritated and our conversation ended rather abruptly. I believe that this kind of intolerance to critical thinking is unhealthy and only perpetuates narrow-mindedness.

Indeed, I believe fundamentalism in Barbados is to some extent responsible for the apparent inability of increasing numbers of our people to reason, and a consequent increase of materialism and violent behavior in this country - again, the youth are a key concern here.

Fundamentalism encourages the type of rash judgment and behavior that fuels misunderstandings, irrational actions and conflict.

The characteristically emotional and sensationalist fervor of North American Evangelical preaching, which virtually sets the pace for fundamentalist practice in the Caribbean - perhaps globally - comes to mind here. This is of course related to the Americans' preoccupation with hype and extreme excitement generally. American television programs such as "Ghostbusters Extreme" exploit this preoccupation among the youth.

At the very least I hope this book encourages Christians to give more relaxed, patient and serious thought to their faith. I hope this book encourages them to seek to composedly and comprehensively

34

inform their faith, as I have been doing for the past several years.

Being "a fool for God" is not wise, if it is just mental laziness or disorganization in disguise. Intellectual indifference, disorganization or laziness is at least as bad as the intellectual arrogance that some persons unjustly accuse me of.

The accusations are unjust because I am not advocating the pursuit of knowledge for its own sake. My position is that the more you put on the line, for the sake of Christ, the more thoroughly you will, (or should) "study to show yourself approved", so as to justify and safeguard your investment in and service to him.

This was and still is the motivation behind my quest for knowledge.

Part of the problem no doubt, is that too many Christians do not take their Christianity seriously enough, or else, are caught up in an overly subjective, predominantly emotional, infatuation-based experience of Jesus, the Bible and the Church.

In this state and frame of mind, these Christians never give serious thought to or inquire after the historical Jesus. They know very little of the history of the Bible and the Church.

Yet it should be apparent to all that such knowledge is indispensable to those who set out to truly give themselves to the Christian cause.

Too many Christians are content to let their leaders do their thinking for them. Again, you need only recall the Jim Jones or David Koresh sagas to see how dangerous that is.

We need to be more self sufficient and individualistic in our reasoning - while of course, at the same time respecting and taking others' views seriously. There must be balance; we must be rational and tolerant.

Fundamentalist Christians should read more widely, particularly to see what other branches of the Church have to say about their own beliefs, not what fundamentalist preachers and commentators are saying about them.

Theologians, bible scholars and other persons who may not hold fundamentalist views about the Bible are not all (nor predominantly) infidels, atheists or haters of God. That is a fundamentalist bogey; part of the inoculation I referred to earlier.

Scholarly critics of the Bible are usually just responding honestly

35

and conscientiously to the evidence with which they are faced, and as they understand it.

The latter point is also made in professor Barr's book. I have drawn on this resource considerably here. I should point out though, that much of the information used in this book has actually been garnered from sources that are largely or wholly of fundamentalist origin - the encyclopedias, commentaries and other texts to which I referred earlier.

I have been pleasantly surprised and made optimistic by the level of openness and objectivity evident in some of these sources, particularly, The International Standard Bible Encyclopedia[5] (subsequently ISBE) of which the General Editor, Professor G.W. Bromiley is Anglican.

Still, it must be said that while making some concessions in the course of their arguments, these texts are not so forthcoming and conciliatory in their conclusions. This type of duality and ambiguity in contemporary biblical scholarship is just one indication of the complexity of the issues that have surfaced in recent times, as our knowledge of the Bible and church history, and of other religions generally, has expanded substantially.

It underscores the need for diligence and patience in Bible study. The simplistic, hasty and rash, "cowboy" style conclusions of fundamentalism must be avoided. Such conclusions are the root of fundamentalist intolerance. This presumptuousness severely limits fundamentalists' ability to empathize with persons who do not share their views.

One thing that has come home to me very forcefully as a result of my own studies, is the inevitability of differing opinions and some uncertainty in Christian belief. The very nature of the biblical evidence dictates this.

Students of the Bible must therefore not allow themselves to be intimidated or made to feel guilty (as I was) because of their indecision on one issue or another of Christian teaching.

One of the essential weaknesses of fundamentalism is its simplistic insistence on a quality of faith which approximates certainty. It can be seen in the altar call" of evangelical crusades where, after a sermon of forty minutes or so, the preacher compels individuals to put their trust totally and irrevocably in the Jesus of fundamentalism.

This type of brainwashing - that is what it amounts to, however well meant as it may be sometimes - is usually executed with the assistance of various emotional stimuli ranging from soft, sentimental music, to the preacher's loud bellowing about the impending and irreversible damnation of lost souls to a fiery hell!

Of course the success of this "rushed recruiting" is linked to generations of dogmatic religious programming in Christian societies.

Ironically though, that preparatory groundwork for the almost worldwide torrential downpour of this type of Christian "ministry" - which we have seen in recent decades - was not laid by the fundamentalist movement (at least not by the well known fundamentalist groups of our day) but rather by the traditional Churches who now criticize fundamentalism.

The naive confidence in scripture - that fertile soil of simplistic faith which rests upon the minds of so many and is so skillfully cultivated and exploited by contemporary fundamentalism - is the residual fodder of centuries of unquestioning reverence and obedience to the Bible that was demanded and enforced by the Roman Catholics, Anglicans and other traditionalists.

The en vogue by-product of rushed-faith which approximates certainty, scarcely raises an eyebrow in our fast paced, "frozen-food, instant-coffee" modern societies but it has its roots in a lopsided, anti-intellectual view of faith which dates back to the less enlightened era of the dark ages.

Actually, it seems certain that from the inception of Christianity there have been followers of "the Way" who did not recognize that faith has a rational, intellectual dimension, and that faith may be enquiring, or even doubting sometimes - as perhaps in the case of Peter, who according to Matthew 14:31 demonstrated both faith and doubt in a single crisis.

There is also the example of those who saw the risen Christ and yet doubted (Matthew 28:17). In these passages the Greek *distazo*, "to stand divided" is used and points to provisional doubt, that is, the doubt of one who is waiting for more light[6].

Fundamentalism's simplistic insistence on "faith", that is certainty, is also fuelled by its teaching on the "plain meaning" of the Bible. The American organization Fundamentalists Anonymous (now defunct, apparently) that seeks to help persons emerging from fundamentalist groups, cites an inability to cope with the ambiguities of life as characteristic of fundamentalism.

This inability is at the heart of the "plain meaning" claim. I shall say more on the notion of the "plain meaning" of the Bible in the next chapter.

Before I conclude this rather lengthy introduction though, I must direct readers attention to what in my view has been the greatest reward of my perseverance in analytical and objective Bible study; my discovery of the true nature and purpose of the New Covenant.

The most significant benefit of my studied encounter with fundamentalism has been my recognition of the virtual oneness of the phenomenon which the Bible identifies as the New Covenant - the law written in our hearts - and the common, very human phenomenon of conscience.

You see, as a fundamentalist, I used to think this New Covenant was written in the Bible. Specifically, I used to think it was identical to, or at least the equivalent of the so-called "New Testament".

Well, persistent analysis of the Bible brought me to the place where I realized that while these two things are obviously related, they are nonetheless very different. My research suggests that the confusion of the two of them occurred in the formative years of the Church.

I spoke to an eminent Anglican scholar about this past confusion of mine, and suggested that this deeply rooted misconception is widely held throughout Christendom.

He disagreed. He did not think the leaders of the early church had committed such an error and he seemed to suggest that if this confusion existed on a large scale at all, it may only exist within fundamentalism, and that there are not that many fundamentalists within Christendom.

I do not know how he has arrived at his estimate of the number of Christians that subscribe to fundamentalism but according to The History of Christianity[7], (subsequently THC) Pentecostals, just one of the many fundamentalist groups, are not merely another denomination or Protestant sect but actually represent

a fourth major strand of Christianity - alongside Orthodoxy, Roman Catholicism and Protestantism.

So even if Pentecostals were the only ones laboring under this delusion (and they are not), that would still be a matter of considerable concern.

Regarding the substantive issue though, I maintain that the early Church leaders are to be held responsible for this error, and that while fundamentalism or other strains of Christianity may not be teaching that the New Covenant and the "New Testament" are the same explicitly (actually, I do not recall being exposed to any really serious or in-depth study on this important concept) this very thing has been implied throughout Christendom almost from its inception.

I am convinced that the labeling of a collection of church writings as the "New Testament" in the second century A.D., has led to the disastrous, virtually universal confusion of the unwritten, individualistic phenomenon that is the New Covenant with that collection of writings - the "New Testament".

The courageous, objective approach to Bible study which I have embraced and am advocating here, has enabled me to see this confusion as a historically entrenched error which has resulted in the devaluation and obscuring of the phenomenon of conscience - of which the New Covenant is, for all intents and purposes, simply a socio-culturally conditioned ancient Jewish and probably wider-Afro-Asiatic metaphor.

I see this confusion as resulting in a tragic subordination of the role of individual conscience - as a significant interpreter and judge of private and public morality - to the role of the Bible or, more specifically its ecclesiastical interpreters.

This error stands as an obstacle to and perverts the inevitable, individualistic pursuit of truth that is a basic function of conscience.

Having gained a clearer understanding of the workings of conscience, I have identified this individualistic pursuit of truth as one of its most important functions - in some cases its most important function.

This pursuit, which is precisely what I am seeking to promote here, is exemplified in the history of the church by persons like Rene Descartes and, to a lesser extent, Martin Luther (my difficulty with Luther as a model is made clear in chapter four).

Consider the following observation, also made in THC[8], regarding

Luther and Descartes, two prominent churchmen who, interestingly, are seen by fundamentalist authorities as representing opposing forces in the history of the church - Descartes is usually represented as a liberal rationalist and philosopher who opposed the church, while Luther is projected as a conservative man of great faith.

> The larger-than-life figures of Descartes and Luther typify the forces that were at work in the seventeenth and eighteenth centuries. They had in common the awareness that we must each make up our own mind. It is useless to accept anyone else's answer as true unless we have proved it for ourselves.

It is my view that the optimum operation of conscience is its self-oriented, individualistic revelation of truth.

This book is therefore dedicated to persons whose first priority is truthfulness to themselves: those of us who know the value of a clear conscience. This, I have come to realize, is what the New Covenant principle is all about.

The confusion of the internally-oriented (private), New Covenant with the externally-oriented (public), written guidelines on morality and truth that constitutes the "New Testament", compromises and obscures this essential individualistic dimension of Jesus' teaching.

The New Covenant, that is conscience, informs "published" guidelines on morality and truth - including those expressed in the "New Testament", and the rest of the Bible.

It is certain that the individual consciences' dicta, the respective etchings of the New Covenant on the hearts of the biblical writers, played a pivotal role in the determination of what they wrote. However, this does not justify the confusion of the New Covenant with the "New Testament".

This confusion is a cornerstone in the unfortunate historical and psychological construct that is the terror of the Bible. It must be exposed and eradicated if the principle of freedom of conscience and individual autonomy that is represented by the biblical concept of the New Covenant and which is key to a full appreciation of the Bible's beauty, is to be more widely embraced by the church and thrive among Christians.

The priority of this individual autonomy must of course be balanced with the reality and workings of social factors - especially the need for social cohesion. There is a possibly infinite tension between these two phenomena which tempts us to view their pursuit as being mutually exclusive.

However, I do not think this is necessarily so. In fact, my own experience has led me to conclude that it is only when the inevitability and validity of differing views on morality among individuals is recognized and accepted, that the need for tolerance, empathy and compassion - the only basis for enduring social cohesion - becomes manifest, and their realization probable.

As I view the unfolding of social relations in my native land Barbados, in the Caribbean region and in the wider world, it seems to me that our best hope for securing enduring, sustainable social cohesion rests on precisely such a recognition and acceptance.

Chapter One
The nature and scope of the problem elaborated

The purpose of this book is twofold. On one hand I am seeking to draw readers' attention to, and discourage the ill-informed, intimidating and ultimately destructive perception of the Bible that I call the terror of the Bible: that perception which makes the Bible a potent instrument of self-abuse in the hands of the ignorant, and a tool of manipulation and exploitation in the hands of the unscrupulous.

On the other hand I hope to encourage a more enlightened and wholesome understanding of the Bible; an understanding whereby both the Bible's strengths and weaknesses are appreciated. An understanding which advances that goal or effect which I like to think is the ultimate goal of the Bible - love of others, as of oneself.

As I noted, the first perception, the 'terror of the Bible', is most evident among fundamentalist Christians such as Baptists, Pentecostals and Wesleyans, on the "orthodox" side, and Jehovah's Witnesses, Mormons and Seventh Day Adventists among "unorthodox" groups, considered cults by "orthodox" fundamentalists.

These and other groups within the evangelical camp claim that the Bible, as a divinely inspired product is "inerrant and infallible". The basic thrust of this claim is that the Bible is a wholly accurate, reliable and trustworthy account and record of God's revelation of Himself to humanity.

Various modifications of this claim have emerged as fundamentalists have sought to respond to increasing critical challenges from the fields of linguistics, archaeology and history.

These modifications range from a redefinition of the term infallible (as in ISBE where, incidentally, the current difficulties involved in explaining the term inerrant are glossed over), to a redirection of the object of this claim, with some fundamentalists now claiming it applies to the original manuscripts of the Bible only - as if that helps.

My concern is with the idealistic, perfectionist concept of inerrancy and infallibility mentioned above. Many of the people who preach the modified concepts follow the perfectionist concept in practice anyway.

It is on the basis of this idealistic concept that fundamentalism proudly cites the Bible as its only authority - the source and foundation of its doctrines and practices. Fundamentalists also use this assertion to distinguish themselves from the older, mostly non-evangelical churches (Roman Catholics, Anglicans, liberal Protestants etc) who subscribe to other authorities - the Pope, church-councils, conscience, reason and so on - along with, and in some ways, exceeding the Bible's authority.

Ironically though, the more notorious fundamentalists' perception of the Bible's divine inspiration - which is the basis for their claims of its inerrancy and infallibility - has been handed down to them by the older mainstream churches, (primarily the Roman Catholic Church) with whom they are constantly at odds. This idealistic perception of the Bible was initially established and defended by Roman Catholics who used allegorical interpretation to get around difficult issues.

Formerly a zealous fundamentalist Christian, and hence inclined to see only the differences in the attitudes of mainstream and fundamentalist churches to the Bible, it took me a while to realize this.

However, an in-depth, literary-historical[1] study of the Bible has convinced me that the intolerance and division-breeding terror of the Bible which characterizes fundamentalism is part of the legacy of the Church Fathers - the first to fourth century leaders of the Church and acknowledged patrons (Saints) of the older, tradition-oriented Churches.

My findings, which as I have noted are based largely on information gathered from fundamentalist sources, have led me to conclude that fundamentalism's assertions are not based on what is actually written in the Bible, as is claimed, but on presumptions about the nature and purpose of the Bible which originated with the Church Fathers.

I have come to the conclusion that it was through the Church Fathers' agency, though perhaps, against their intention, as some may argue[2], that the Bible was initially endowed with the awe-inspiring and intimidating aura of an unquestionable medium of God's truth.

The ancient church leaders, also called "the Fathers", may not have used the terms "inerrant and infallible" to describe scripture, but the implication was there[3].

Of course, a similar attitude to scripture had obtained in Judaism

43

for some time, but the Church Fathers established this idea among Christians. They transferred this perception of the Jewish scriptures onto their own creation - the Bible.

Today the older non-evangelical churches have partly abandoned this idealistic, even idolatrous[4], attitude toward scripture. This, as the Interpreter's Dictionary of the Bible[5] (subsequently IDB) concludes, has coincided with the emergence of the historical-critical view of the Bible:

> For several centuries it was held that the OT (i.e., prophecy and typology) was an authentic 'source' for the life of Jesus. With the prevailing view of the inspiration of scripture, this was natural and inevitable. For several centuries the interpretation of the gospels, and of the Bible generally, from the point of view of systematic or dogmatic theology was unquestioned (Is not all divine truth one?), with the result that the gospels were forced to yield data which could readily be fitted into whatever dogmatic system was held by the commentator or exegete. Only with the rise of the modern historical-critical view of the Bible has the procedure been reversed, and the data of the gospels established first and without regard to the requirements or presuppositions of systematic theology.

Nonetheless, I have noticed signs suggesting that a significant number of persons (both clergy and laity) in the older churches are either unaware of, or have not come to terms with the progress made in modern biblical analysis and interpretation.

It seems that while many individuals and organizations associated with these churches (for example, in Barbados, the Reverends Andrew Hatch, Dr. John Holder and Harcourt Blackett, and institutions like the Caribbean Conference of Churches) are at the forefront of the courageous struggle to promote a historically-justifiable appreciation of the nature and purpose of the Bible, others, for one reason or another, are adopting a more conservative position.

Some of them are taking a position very much like fundamentalism, which pays little or no attention to the historical circumstances in and by which the Bible came into being.

I have been surprised by the level of ignorance and naiveté about matters surrounding the Bible's history that is exhibited in some of these churches whose leaders are usually better informed than fundamentalist pastors and elders.

Actually, I find it difficult to believe that enlightened and liberated leaders of the older churches actually embrace naive fundamentalist views about the Bible, and so I often wonder if they are merely taking fundamentalist positions publicly, in an effort to exploit the wave of popularity that fundamentalists, especially Pentecostal groups, have been enjoying for the past several decades.

In 1996 the regional newspaper Caribbean Week[6] carried a special feature highlighting "A kind of religious war" between the Roman Catholic Church in Brazil and a Pentecostal group called the Universal Church of the Kingdom of God, which has achieved phenomenal success (3.5 million Brazilian adherents, and an estimated annual income of US$1 billion) in this Catholic stronghold - the largest Catholic nation in the world.

This article notes that when Pope John Paul II visited Brazil in October 1991 and held a mass in Brasilia it attracted 100,000 people, while prayer meetings held by the Universal Church attracted a total of 400,000.

The adoption of fundamentalist positions may be some mainstream preachers response to this kind of situation. If it is such a self-serving ploy, it is highly reprehensible and it merely perpetuates the idealism, ignorance and paranoia upon which fundamentalism feeds.

Another more profound and perhaps more sympathetic motivation behind these leaders' adoption or propagation of fundamentalist views may be their justification of such a retrogression as the lesser of two evils: the other *assumed* evil would entail the total disintegration of Christian faith in the face of modern biblical criticism.

Convinced of an intrinsic virtue in the Bible and the church (the existence of these two "institutions" and the manner in which they are perceived being interdependent), these "fundamentalism flirting" mainstream leaders may view fundamentalism as the only means of preserving the Bible and the church as the influential and respectable entities they believe these ancient agents of socialization (or redemption) deserve to be.

45

Beyond all the dissension and quibbling, this kind of conservative reasoning, or self-preserving impulse is the basis of the essential kinship and "unity" between persons in the tradition-oriented churches and their fundamentalist counterparts. This is why I hold both groups responsible for the historically entrenched tyranny and terror of the Bible.

It is only the extent and or occasion of either group's responsibility that is variable.

In a similar manner, Barr identifies a group he refers to as "the evangelical but non-fundamentalist constituency": that is, evangelicals who disassociate themselves from fundamentalism, but much of whose language and terminology is only a diluted and milder form of the basic "fundamentalist conceptuality"[7].

Barr challenges this branch of the Christian collective to make a clean break with fundamentalism. He charges that

> Evangelicalism, if it is to differ from fundamentalism,
> has to work out and assert boldly a theological and
> biblical position that fully abandons the fundamentalist
> ideas.

Like Barr's, my approach here is therefore quite radical. Indeed, at its core, I think it is somewhat more radical than Barr's.

This is not a polemic against any one Christian denomination or grouping. As I indicated before, my use of the term fundamentalist should be construed as applying to all Christians who hold or advocate fundamentalist beliefs, irrespective of their church affiliation.

The erroneous perception of the Bible that I am addressing here may be most plainly manifested among those officially or commonly recognized as fundamentalists, but it is a perception, that is to some degree present in all churches. It is a problem that is rooted in the very conception of the Bible and the church.

In opposition to the fundamentalist superficial preoccupation with scripture which ultimately distorts the truth about the Bible, I shall be discussing literary and historical evidence (much of which is in the Bible itself), which has led me to the conclusion that Jesus[8] of Nazareth did not bequeath his followers the Jewish scriptures, nor any other collection of writings; that he did not intend for his followers to be living and judging themselves and others by a literary code, that is, written communication, of any kind, and that the book called the Bible and the institution called the church are more the creation of the church-fathers than the product of Jesus' teachings.

I shall show you why I am persuaded that humanity's conscience - not the Bible or any church hierarchy - should be recognized as the Christian's, and indeed, all humanity's final authority: our ultimate court of appeal.

Why I believe that the phenomenon of conscience is synonymous with the New Covenant or the mystical "law" written in men's hearts (Hebrews 8:8; Romans2:14,15), the divine-human interaction of spirits spoken of in Romans 8:16, and the "anointing" referred to in 1 John 2:20, 27.

My purpose is not to deter people from reading the Bible, but rather to promote a more courageous and sensible appreciation of it than fundamentalism allows.

Fundamentalists are generally viewed as persons who take the Bible very seriously, even if in a distorted way, (for example, Jim Jones and David Koresh).

I want to make it clear that I take the Bible very seriously too. In fact I consider myself a fundamentalist, that is, a radical, or to use Rastafarian parlance, a *rootical* man, but in a more enlightened, and historically justifiable sense of the word than Koresh and company.

As far as I am concerned Jones and Koresh's brand of fundamentalism was a self-serving sham. It was shallow and superficial, and therefore not fundamentalism at all.

As I mentioned in the introduction, I once embraced the same kind of shallow concept of the Bible's nature, its origin and purpose. I noted that I had been exposed to that perception of scripture as a child - as most Barbadian children were and probably still are. I also subsequently preached that perception of scripture from the roadside in open-air meetings, and virtually everywhere and every time I had the opportunity, and courage to.

As a fundamentalist Christian, I purposed that my life was to be totally dominated and regulated by that concept of the Bible, and the concept of Jesus it engenders. It was the basis of my hopes and dreams; I was willing to submit and surrender myself totally to it.

47

I noted too that it was only as I decided to accept the Bible as it is, that is, as I realized that belief in the integrity of God is not dependent on or otherwise necessarily tied to belief in the "inerrancy and infallibility" of the Bible - that I was relieved of the guilt, anxiety and bewilderment that accompanied the weakening of my fundamentalist convictions.

The point I am making here, is that I still have a zeal for the things of God. I would not be writing this book if I did not. The difference between my zeal and the zeal of others like Koresh, whom I call superficial fundamentalists, is that mine has been tempered by the knowledge of the Bible and church-history which I pursued and acquired (I say this with absolutely no sense of self-acclaim). This acquisition has made my faith more objective.

I no longer approach biblical study armed with the presumptions of fundamentalist doctrine or any other systematic or dogmatic theology - although I have noticed some important parallels between my views on the importance of "immediate experience" and those of others, like the seventeenth century Quakers, led by George Fox[9].

The view of the Bible which I now embrace and am advocating here, is based largely on a literary-historical study of what is actually written in the Bible. I now subscribe significantly to the modern historical-critical view mentioned above.

Unlike fundamentalists I do not purport to follow the "plain meaning" of the Bible, for my studies have convinced me that the meaning of the Bible - if taken at face value - is anything but plain.

This fact is overwhelmingly attested to by the lack of consensus over what the so-called "plain meaning" is, among the various fundamentalist groups which claim to follow it!

I believe a "meaning of the Bible", in whole or in part, cannot be sensibly or accurately assessed apart from an investigation of the circumstances in which the Bible came in to being.

The Bible is an ancient document. Logically, the quest for its meaning entails historical investigation.

Jesus is a historical figure - he lived and acted at a particular time, and in particular circumstances. The relevance of his life to ours must be assessed within the context of the circumstances in which he lived. Those circumstances are a part of distant history, and as such are not as easily assessed as fundamentalists assume.

IDB[10] observes,

> The question is often asked, whether it is possible, on
> the basis of the tradition contained in the gospels, to
> write a life of Jesus. The diversity - in fact, the total
> disagreement - of the lives of Jesus produced during the
> past two centuries does not encourage optimism.

Efforts to produce Jesus' biography have apparently only managed
to convince scholars of the difficulties involved in such an
undertaking. IDB further remarks

> it is now more clearly recognized than ever before
> that the student needs a fuller equipment of knowledge
> than has sometimes been the case, and cannot trust to his
> own private and personal impressions derived from the
> careful reading of the English Bible.
> He needs ancient languages, and also should be
> familiar with ancient literature and history, not only
> classical but also Semitic, for the gospels contain
> originally Semitic (i.e., Aramaic) traditions in Greek
> translation; he should also be familiar with ancient
> historiography and realize that there are questions which
> it is useless to ask...it will have to be recognized that we
> shall probably never get back to a fully detailed,
> photographically authentic account of Jesus' life and
> character and to tape-recorded accuracy in the
> reproduction of his sayings.

An essential error of shallow fundamentalist biblical interpretation
is its scant respect, or else, blatant disregard for the historical context
in which the books of the Bible (particularly the so-called "New
Testament") were written and compiled.

Many of their preachers are unaware (some, perhaps, conveniently
forget) that the sayings attributed to Jesus in the Bible are "traditions",
that is, sayings handed down by his followers, not verbatim records[11].

I have noticed that in this current age of technological
advancement and the "information boom", it has become fashionable

for fundamentalists to show a concern with the historical context of scripture. Hence some fundamentalist preachers are now paying some attention to the immediate circumstances in which their chosen text was written - when, where, by whom, to whom and so on.

However, in the average fundamentalist sermon, this concern is always limited by and subordinated to the preachers' ill-founded dogma.

Hence, for example, none of the serious questions that surround the authorship and dating of the four gospels and many of the epistles are raised.

The fundamentalist preacher's method is predominantly (in some cases, purely) a literal method of interpretation which, in practice, operates on the assumption that the divine inspiration of scripture excludes it from or elevates it above serious, that is, critical, historical questioning or investigation.

Fundamentalists generally view such research as a non-spiritual ("fleshy") and faithless questioning of the word of God. Despite all their assertions about the power and sovereignty of God, they apparently have difficulty seeing how the Almighty could have operated within the natural processes of history to produce the Bible.

This is just part of what I call a perfectionist dilemma; a lack of faith in the ability of God to perform his will within the fallible processes of history. It is a part of the idealism of fundamentalists - that longing for an infallible guide that I referred to earlier.

I believe that this idealism, perhaps combined with unconscious or deliberate dishonesty, power-hunger and greed, is behind the recent emergence of the so-called "Torah Code" among Jews and the "Bible Code", among Christians.

These codes, which essentially reduce scientific research into the Bible to a speculative "numbers game", demonstrate the extent of Jewish and Christian fundamentalists' determination to preserve their idealistic perception of their scriptures.

The codes undermine the democratic, populist gains in Bible study that have been made by scholarly groups like the "Jesus Seminar" of the USA and subtly move serious Bible study back under the dominion of an elite class - in this case statisticians.

In my opinion, the codes are religion dominating, masses exploiting tools which fundamentalist leaders are resorting to because

50

they sense that with the advance of the information age, the traditional anti-intellectual and anti-scientific arguments for the inspiration, inerrancy and infallibility of the Bible are not being as successful as before.

Therefore, in opposition to fundamentalists' insistence that their declaration of the "inerrancy and infallibility" of the Bible demonstrates great faith in God, I am suggesting that it takes greater faith and confidence in God, to believe that he can accomplish his will in spite of the handicap of an errant and fallible Bible.

This is the quality of faith that I embrace. It is a faith in God that sees him[11] operating in the past, present and future in and in spite of human failings.

It is a freedom from anxiety, an abandonment or surrender, that comes with the assurance that God's sovereignty encompasses all history - the good and the bad - and yet ensures the triumph of the good.

It should be clear to the reader that while my faith has been radically altered by the revelations of modern biblical research, it has not been extinguished by them.

This faith, a victorious faith, is the basis of the optimism with which I prepare this discourse. I write with the confidence that the terror of the Bible can be overcome and a historically grounded appreciation of its beauty articulated.

I do not believe that the relegation of the Bible in church administration to a "lesser" status than that on which fundamentalists insist, will induce the moral decay and breakdown of law and order that they characteristically seem to fear.

On the contrary, I believe that precisely such a rationalization of the Bible's worth is necessary if there is to be any meaningful resolution of the differences which now fragment churches, families and entire nations - differences which in fact contribute to moral decay and the breakdown of law and order.

I truly anticipate meaningful reform and reconciliation throughout Christendom - and even between Christians and those who embrace other faiths - as we retrace our steps and seek in the present and future, to make up for past errors and failures.

It is in retracing our steps, that is, re-exploring the roots of our various faiths that we will discover all that we have in common.

51

In this conciliatory spirit, I challenge readers to overcome the terror of the Bible, and I commend the approach to the Bible advocated here as a compelling option by which Christians, and indeed, all humanity can be uplifted and enriched.

As a point of departure in this direction, the next chapter demonstrates the weakness of the fundamentalist doctrine of the inerrancy and infallibility of the Bible from none other than a biblical perspective.

Chapter Two
The doctrine of inerrancy
and infallibility examined

Basic to the fundamentalist position is their argument that the Bible is inerrant and infallible; that it is wholly accurate and consistent - both historically and in its themes.

Fundamentalists, most of whom probably mean well, insist that this view of the Bible is advocated by the Bible itself, particularly the passages 2 Timothy 3:16 and 2 Peter 1:19-21 which they believe speak of the "inspiration" of the Bible.

Fundamentalists therefore argue that they are merely agreeing with the Bible's "self-witness" and speak of the Bible as "self-interpreting". This is what fundamentalists mean when insisting that they are following the "plain meaning" of the Bible.

These claims simply are not factual though, however sincerely they may be stated. This chapter is devoted to a consideration of 2 Timothy 3:16 and 2 Peter 1:19-21 - the fundamentalists' scriptural support for their twin doctrines of the inerrancy and infallibility of the Bible and its final or supreme authority in Christianity.

It shall be seen that when properly translated and put in their literary and historical contexts, the passages cited by fundamentalists actually undermine their position, and in fact offer greater, or at least equal support, to other strains of Christianity.

The main passage of scripture used by fundamentalists is 2 Timothy 3:16, which according to the King James Version (KJV), reads

> All scripture is given by inspiration of God, and is profitable for doctrine, for reproof, for correction, for instruction in righteousness:

We will begin our study of this passage by examining the first section, which says "All scripture is given by inspiration of God..." There are just three Greek words behind this translation, "*Pasa graphe theopneustos"*

First of all, I want to draw your attention to the fact that these words are not referring to the Bible.

The Greek word *pasa* is translated "All" in the King James version, but *pasa* is employed distributively here and is actually referring specifically to that scripture (*graphe*) already mentioned in verse 15, that is, "the holy scriptures" (see Eerdmans New Bible Commentary).

A better translation of the first phrase in this passage would therefore be, "All these scriptures", meaning those mentioned in verse 15, "the holy scriptures".

Now, the Greek phrase translated "the holy scriptures" in verse 15 is *te gramma*. This phrase does not refer to the Bible. The Greek word behind Bible is *biblia*, which originally meant "books"[1] (not "book").

On its own, *gramma* also means "books", but combined with the definite article *te* as in 2 Timothy 3:15, it is a virtual technical term which refers exclusively to the sacred writings of Judaism, that is, "the law and the prophets". Following an error in the Septuagint[2], namely the use of the Greek *diatheke*, for the Hebrew *berit*[3], Christians have called this portion of scripture the "Old Testament".

The Greek term *Te gramma* is used in this way in the writings of Philo and Josephus, two prominent Jewish figures in the first and second centuries.

2 Timothy 3:16 is therefore referring to the Jewish writings, not the Bible, as fundamentalists assume.

This is an important point that has not only been overlooked by the obviously fundamentalist Christian groups, but by many other Christians worldwide, who embrace a simplistic view of the Bible's origin; a simplistic view of the Bible's "inspiration".

The average Christian - a Christian who has not been exposed to any systematic literary-historical study of the Bible - tends to think that the Bible, which is a combination of two canons of scripture (the Jewish and Christian canons) always existed as a single canon of scriptures, or that the two canons which now comprise it were divinely ordained, naturally destined or in some similar fashion *inevitably intended* to become one.

These Christians have no sense or inkling of the mundane historical processes that brought the Jewish and Christian scriptures

54

together as "one" canon. They know little or nothing about the complex, conflict-plagued relationship that existed between first and second century Jews and Christians - most of the latter being converts from Judaism initially - and how this relationship influenced the creation of the "one" canon of scripture we know as the Bible.

Consequently, these Christians generally assume that all of Jesus' and the disciples' references to "scripture" in the Bible are references to the Bible itself. This is far from true.

The Bible did not exist in Jesus' time. The Bible only came into being when the Jewish scriptures ("Old Testament") were combined with the collection of Christian writings that was called the "New Testament". It is doubtful that Jesus of Nazareth either foresaw or intended the combination of these two bodies of scripture, not least of all, because it is virtually certain that Jesus neither intended nor foresaw the existence of the so-called "New Testament".

I noted earlier that the "New Testament" represents a confusion of authoritative Christian writings with the unwritten authoritative phenomenon called the New Covenant. The use of the literalistic term "Testament" (Greek diatheke) in reference to both the old and the new covenant writings, has only helped to confuse the issue.

The fact is, the Bible came into being (more or less) when the Jewish scriptures were officially combined with Christian writings (gospels, epistles etc) which had been misleadingly identified with the New Covenant, sometime between 196 and 212 AD.

The misleading identification of these writings with the New Covenant, preceded and (in conjunction with other developments to be discussed subsequently) led to the creation of the Bible.

Nowhere in the Bible is it suggested that Jesus or any of the apostles ever referred to any written material as the New Covenant (or "New Testament" for that matter).

According to the Bible itself, the New Covenant is an unwritten, spiritual phenomenon.

Jeremiah 31:31-34, describes the New Covenant as a non-literal, invisible dynamic: a heart or conscience oriented, authoritative covenant which God promised to implement in place of the written, visible Mosaic covenant, which was based on the law and had proven defective.

It is this New Covenant (according to the RV; the AV has "New

Testament") that Jesus is identified with in Matthew 26:28, Mark 14:24, and Luke 22:20.

It is this New Covenant that the author is referring to in Hebrews 8:6,8,10,13; 10:16,29; 12:24; and 13:20.

Apparently, it was the church-father Tertullian, whose surviving works date from between 196 and 212 AD who first referred to written materials as the "New Testament", Latin *novum testamentum*.

By so doing, he either initiated the confusion of the New Covenant with written matter or else, through his sanction as a recognized leader in the early church, made official this confusion which may have already existed in the minds of many Christians - as a result of their preoccupation with these scriptures.

So then, at the time it occurred, the combination of the Jewish and Christian scriptures was neither a natural nor inevitable development because it occurred in conjunction with the catastrophic confusion of the "New Testament" writings with the unwritten authoritative phenomenon called the New Covenant.

Like this unfortunate obscuring of the identity, nature and purpose of the New Covenant, the combining of the Jewish and Christian scriptures will therefore be seen to have probably undermined Jesus' mission.

The main concern now though, is simply for the reader to recognize that the claims in 2 Timothy 3:16 are made for the Jewish scriptures only.

And what exactly are these claims? This is the focus of my second point.

Is there, as fundamentalists insist, a suggestion here that the scriptures referred to are "inerrant and infallible"? Judging by what is actually written in this verse, I would have to say no.

The only thing claimed for the scriptures concerned here (the Jewish scriptures), is their profitability. The author of this verse simply suggests that an element of divine involvement in the creation of the Jewish scriptures makes them profitable - for reproof, correction etc.

Now, the element of divine involvement - which is really the basis of Christian fundamentalists' "hysteria" - is signified by the use of the Greek term *theopneustos*, which the King James translators have rendered, "given by the inspiration of God".

However, *theopneustos* does not speak of inspiring or inspiration. It does not suggest that God breathed into scripture or its authors, but merely that he breathed-out, that is, he exhaled (see INSPIRATION, II. Relevant Passages ISBE).

The most that can be affirmed by the use of *theopneustos* in 2 Timothy 3:16 therefore, is that there is some essential relationship between God's breathing-out and scripture. The precise nature of this relationship is not discussed.

ISBE[4] makes the same point. Ironically, but not surprisingly, the point about the passage's vagueness is made while defending the fundamentalist position:

> In a word, what is declared by this fundamental passage is simply that the scriptures are a divine product, without any indication of how God has operated in producing them.

My question is, why are fundamentalists claiming that the mention of such an obscure relationship between divine activity and the origin of scripture suggests that scripture is "inerrant and infallible"?

Or, it may be more effectively put this way. If the use of *theopneustos* in 2 Timothy 3:16 obliges us to conclude that the scriptures concerned are "inerrant and infallible", doesn't Genesis 2:7 oblige us to conclude that man himself is "inerrant and infallible"? !

This passage reads:

> And the lord God formed man of the dust of the ground, and breathed into his nostrils the breath of life.

The Hebrew terms employed here (*naphach* = breathed, and *el* = into) suggest inspiration in the truest, most explicit and exalted sense of the word imaginable.

Why then, are fundamentalists not arguing that man is inerrant and infallible?

Fundamentalists cannot even argue that humanity was inerrant and infallible before "the fall" of Adam and Eve, because on one hand, that would make original man equal with God (which they cannot accept), and on the other, it would suggest that the inerrant can err and

57

the infallible can fail. This is a contradiction, and at the very least undermines fundamentalists' view of inerrancy and infallibility.

We all know that humanity is both errant and fallible, and the suggestion that we are the divinely inbreathed or inspired creation of God has not blinded anyone (except perhaps, an old girlfriend of mine) to this fact.

Fundamentalists accept that God's express inspiration of humanity has not made us flawless - indeed, they seem to think most of us are destined for eternal destruction.

Why then do they regard the obscure suggestion of divine involvement in the creation of scripture as an indication and guarantee that it is inerrant and infallible?

The use of the word *theopneustos* does not require such a conclusion. This word does not even speak of inspiration in the most natural sense of the word!

The fundamentalist assumption (and it is no more than an assumption, however well intentioned) that scripture's origination in divine activity makes it inerrant and infallible, cannot be substantiated by what is written in 2 Timothy 3:16. The claim of the Bible's inerrancy and infallibility is, among other things, a hasty and ill-conceived reaction to the suggestion that the Jewish scriptures are "God-breathed".

The biblical author made no claim of inerrancy or infallibility. The passage simply claims that the scriptures concerned are profitable.

This, as Barr, points out[5], is a very low key assertion. He comments,

> What the passage does not say is that scripture, being inspired, is the controlling and dominating criterion for the nature and character of the Christian faith.

Yet this is exactly how those who use this passage to argue that scripture is inerrant and infallible and consequently, the supreme and final authority in the church, interpret and expound it. They make the profitability of scripture an absolute. The biblical writer did not go that far. In fact, there is evidence which suggests that the writer was very much aware that the profitability of the scriptures concerned was *relative*.

I draw your attention to 2 Corinthians 3:6 which, according to fundamentalist teaching, was written by the same author, the apostle Paul. Here reference is also made to *te gramma*.

This time though, it is translated "the letter", not "the holy scriptures", because the King James translators probably did not want readers of the Bible to know that it is the same scriptures which are praised in 2 Timothy 3:16, that are being denounced here.

They were apparently seeking to preserve that idealistic perception of the scriptures - the intimidating, obedience and submission engendering "terror" of it - which had long been established by their time.

According to them therefore, the author declares that Christ has made himself (the apostle) and others,

> ..able ministers of the New Covenant; not of the letter,
> but of the spirit: for the letter killeth, but the spirit giveth
> life.

However, a more objective and accurate reading of this passage would be achieved if, in keeping with the basic and standard principle of consistency in biblical translation, *te gramma* was translated "the scriptures" as in 2 Timothy 3:15. This passage would therefore read:

> ...able ministers of the New Covenant; not of the scriptures, but of
> the spirit: for the scriptures killeth, but the spirit giveth life."

This rendering may seem shocking at first, but in the context of the Christian-Jewish antagonism that existed in the first and second centuries it is probable.

The main point though, is that it is wholly reconcilable with the claim that these scriptures are profitable, when that profitability is seen as a relative quality, not an absolute condition.

Using fire as an analogy, one can easily see how that which may be profitable - when used to light our paths and to provide warmth and nourishment for us - can also be a terror and the means by which we may destroy ourselves and others. The notorious David Koresh inferno at Waco, Texas in 1993, has demonstrated this beyond the limits of metaphor.

There is therefore no contradiction, and hardly a paradox, between 2 Timothy 3:16 and 2 Corinthians 3:6 when these two verses are properly translated and understood (I am not suggesting that there are no contradictions on the same or other subjects elsewhere in the Bible).

The claim that the Jewish scriptures "killeth" is only made inconsistent with the claim that they are "profitable" when one insists that their profitability is absolute. In other words, that they are inerrant and infallible, in the traditional fundamentalist sense of these terms.

The author of 2 Timothy 3:16 makes no such claim. He evidently held a more balanced opinion of scripture.

Actually, the words inerrant and infallible do not even appear in the Bible. These, as ISBE concedes, are theological rather than biblical expressions.

What is more, the term "inerrant" does not appear in any of the earliest church creeds, and the earliest usage of "infallible" seems to have been by Thomas Aquinas (1225-1274) who applied this term to God's grace[6], not the Bible.

Initially, the Reformers also employed "infallible" to express certainty of the efficacy of God's grace. Their earliest application of "infallible" to the Bible seems to have been in the Belgic Confession (1570s).

Of course, unbalanced, idealistic views about the Bible were present in the church prior to the employment of the term "infallible" to refer to it. As I mentioned in the previous chapter, these ideas can be traced to the influence of conservative, literalistic Judaism on Christianity, that is, fundamentalist Jews' excessive reverence of the "law and the prophets". I deal with this more extensively in the next chapter.

Digressing slightly, I must note that at a deeper level - as a feature of religions generally - this type of "infatuated reverence" for authoritative objects has its roots in the already identified psychological longing of man for an unquestionable, unchanging guide to life.

I must also note that literary guides tend to satisfy this longing because of the "fixed" character of written material. Consider many Muslims' attitude to the Koran.

60

There are traces of this extreme, conservative and literalistic impulse in many parts of the New Testament (particularly the gospel according to Matthew[7]) but not in 2 Timothy 3:16.

The author's affirmation of the profitability of scripture here is set in moderate language, and besides this, appears almost incidentally.

This brings me to my third point: the fact that when this epistle is studied as a whole, one finds that the passage which fundamentalists treat as its central theme and a cornerstone of the Christian faith does not occupy such a pivotal position in the "New Testament".

This epistle, along with 1Timothy and Titus are known as the Pastoral Epistles because their primary interest is the preservation and continuity of the church through carefully appointed leadership and the maintenance of order.

The author states in 1 Timothy 3:14,15 that he is writing with the intention of seeing Timothy shortly, but failing this,

> that thou mayest know how thou oughtest to behave
> thyself in the house of God, which is the church of the
> living God...

In this regard direction is given in these epistles concerning the personal qualities of bishops and deacons, the conduct of various groups (young women, widows, the wealthy etc), matters of church discipline, the treatment of heresies and the like.

Fundamental to and foremost among all these directives is the solemn admonition found in 2 Timothy 1:13, 14, which says

> Hold fast the form of sound words, which thou hast
> heard of me, in faith and love which is in Christ Jesus.
> That good thing which was committed unto thee keep by
> the Holy Ghost which dwelleth in us.

The same charge was stated poignantly and in earnest towards the conclusion of the first epistle (1 Timothy 6:20):

> O Timothy, keep that which was committed to thy
> trust,..

In these passages, the author is referring to a specific pattern or formula of oral teaching, by which the gospel was passed on and preserved.

This oral formula came to be known as the "deposit" - Greek *parakatatheke* or, in later versions of Textus Receptus[8], paratheke - a trust, presumably committed by Christ to his disciples and from them onward.

This is the "form of doctrine" spoken of in Romans 6:17. It was, as this verse suggests, a form of tradition; that is to say, the Greek verb *paradidomi*, translated "delivered" here, signifies the transmission of teaching as tradition.

There is therefore some basis to the Roman Catholic and other mainstream churches' preoccupation with tradition, and it is ironic that the very epistle used by fundamentalists to refute Roman Catholic arguments for the authority of tradition should bear this out, a point also made by Barr.

I will say more about the role of tradition in primitive Christianity shortly. The point I want the reader to grasp here, is that fundamentalists overrate the importance of 2 Timothy 3:16 to the entire epistle. The main subject of this epistle is the transmission of Jesus teaching via oral tradition, not scripture.

Now, the fundamentalist Wycliffe Bible Commentary identifies 2 Timothy 1:14 as the heart of the Pastoral Epistles. However, that publication suggests that the "deposit" is a written record - blatantly ignoring verse 13, which makes it clear that "that good thing" is what Timothy has "heard".

In only too typical literalistic fundamentalist fashion, the Wycliffe Commentary thereby rejects the plain meaning of this verse, in order to preserve and promote the fundamentalist preoccupation with scripture. This is unacceptable by the fundamentalists' own standards.

Clearly the deposit is what Timothy has heard, not what he has read!

Actually, and I am sure that this will come as a surprise to many of my fundamentalist friends, it has long been recognized that in the earliest stages of the "Jesus movement", oral tradition dominated the transmission of the gospel and the role of scripture was secondary.

The very word translated "gospel" attests to this fact. The Greek term *euagellion*, translated "gospel" originally signified an oral declaration. ISBE[9] notes that in the days of the apostles, the verb *euagelizomai* ("proclaim the good news") signified

> the activity of public or private speaking or else believing or receiving, but not writing or reading.

The use of *euagelizomai* in the sense of written documents (e.g. "the four gospels") was much later, first found in Justin Martyr's (Martyr died AD 165) description of a liturgical service at which "the memoirs of the apostles...called gospels were read (Apoli.66)".

Informed biblical scholarship is generally agreed that oral tradition was the very first means by which Jesus' teachings were transmitted.

In its article on tradition the fundamentalist ISBE clearly concedes this:

> Comparisons with contemporary techniques of Jewish teaching and transmission suggest that the teachers passed on the oral texts by reciting them over and over again until those who heard could recite them flawlessly from memory.

Suggesting how these oral traditions may have been converted to written form initially, ISBE goes on,

> It is likely that some records were soon made; notebooks and secret scrolls would have been used as aids to the memory. In this way small collections of traditions about Jesus would have emerged.

In the prologue to the "gospel" attributed to Luke[10] the author clearly states that he was about to use such oral traditions which had been "delivered" (*paradidomi*) to himself and others.

So, there can be no doubt that there was an authoritative oral tradition which preceded the Church's writings and on which these writings are based.

Let me point out here that I am not suggesting that this oral teaching should be substituted for the Bible as another inerrant and infallible, final authority - the criterion of Christian dogma and practice.

As I indicated earlier, I believe the Christian's final authority should be the law written in one's heart, that is, conscience, or in Judeo-Christian terms, the New Covenant. I give this internal authoritative phenomenon precedence over both the oral and written, externally-oriented authoritative mediums of the church. In fact I see both the scriptures and the oral teachings on which they are based as outer-tradition (to be distinguished from inner-tradition) and hence secondary[11].

My point, quite simply, is that the pastoral epistles are mainly concerned with the faithful transmission and preservation of Jesus' teaching through oral tradition, not scripture

The mention of the Jewish scriptures in 2 Timothy 3:16 is in fact secondary. These scriptures are mentioned in relation to their usefulness to "the man of God" (verse 17): the man with whom the truth was deposited, via the oral tradition, and who is responsible for depositing that truth, presumably via the same oral medium, with others deemed worthy (2 Timothy 2:2).

As in Catholicism and other tradition-oriented branches of Christianity, men, not scripture, are viewed as God's intended repository of truth (the issue of gender prejudice in Judaism, Christianity and Catholicism is an important one but I take that up elsewhere).

The fact that attention is given to scripture at all, may be evidence that some of the factors which eventually led to its virtual deification were already in operation.

Still, there is no justification for the fundamentalist treatment of 2 Timothy 3:16 as the central statement of this epistle, or a proof text for their assumptions about scripture. As Barr notes[12] at the conclusion of his study of 2 Timothy 3:16

>..the letter to Timothy makes it clear that the
>inspiration of scripture is a significant concept in the
>mind of the writer. Because the sacred writings -
>undefined[13] - are inspired, they can be relied on to build
>up the reader in the Christian life and to supply his needs.
>But no implications about the inerrancy and infallibility
>of scripture are expressed, and there is no sign that the

inspiration of scripture is for him the keystone of the church...When the passage is used as a proof for ideas of inerrancy and infallibility, or the idea that the "doctrine of scripture" is the foundation charter of the church therefore, this can be done, and is done, only by reading into the passage ideas that were not at all in the mind of the writer and, to that extent, by denying the truth of the passage itself.

We may now recap the main points of the preceding discussion.

First of all I have made the point that 2 Timothy 3:16 does not refer to the Bible, but rather to the Jewish scriptures only. While making this point, I have also sought to draw readers' attention to the fact that the Bible was conceived in and owes its existence largely to an error initiated by the church-father Tertullian, namely, the confusion of the New Covenant with the collection of church writings called the "New Testament". I believe this latter point is of a significance much like that of Columbus' rediscovery of the New World! So profound and far reaching can be its impact on the way the mission of Jesus is interpreted.

Following this, I made the point that there is no claim of inerrancy or infallibility in 2 Timothy 3:16 - that this verse merely describes the scriptures concerned as profitable. Like Barr, I suggested that the fundamentalist claims are merely an overreaction to the author's use of the term *theopneustos* which links the origin of scripture to divine activity.

I suggested that if the use of *theopneustos* is regarded as proof of scripture's inerrancy and infallibility, then the mention of a clearer and more profound link between divine activity and the origin of man in Genesis 2:7 should be regarded as proof of the inerrancy and infallibility of man.

I also sought to show the reader that the author of 2Timothy viewed the profitability of scripture as a relative quality, not an absolute condition.

Thirdly, I demonstrated that within the context of the entire epistle, the profitability of scripture is mentioned almost as an aside. I sought to show readers that the main concern of the author of 2 Timothy is the transmission and preservation of Christ's teachings in a particular oral tradition and that 2 Timothy 3:16 therefore gives more support to the Catholic and mainstream position than it does to the fundamentalists'.

Let us now look briefly at 2 Peter 1:19-21, the other passage that is frequently cited by fundamentalists to support their interpretation of the Bible's "self witness".
This verse reads,

> We have also a more sure word of prophecy;
> whereunto ye do well that ye take heed, as unto a light
> that shineth in a dark place, until the day dawn, and the
> day star arise in your hearts: knowing this first, that no
> prophecy of scripture is of any private interpretation. For
> the prophecy came not by the will of man: but holy men
> of God spake as they were moved by the holy ghost.

Now trustworthiness is an issue here, at least in verse 19, and this calls to mind the idea of inerrancy and infallibility, even though these terms are not used.

However while fundamentalists view this verse as arguing that scripture is more reliable than the voice from heaven (verses 17 and 18), it may be better interpreted as saying that the fulfillment of events by Jesus' first coming make belief in other prophecies about him easier.

According to this understanding (advocated by Eerdman's New Bible Commentary[14]), historical fulfillment is the basis of the trustworthiness advocated - not the mere prophesying of events in scripture.

The writer of the epistle is not saying that the prophecies of scripture are certain because they are scripture, but rather that the fulfillment in history of some of scripture's prophecies suggests that the ones yet unfulfilled are reliable.

Hence, the Amplified Bible, attempting to convey the critical role of historical fulfillment, renders this verse

> And we have the prophetic word [made] firmer still;

that is, made more convincing by the prior fulfillment of other prophecies. This is an appeal to objective evidence, not the intrinsic trustworthiness of scripture that fundamentalists advocate.

The subsequent presentation of Christ's second coming as a subjective, spiritual reality which occurs in believers' hearts (which, by the way, recalls the New Covenant phenomenon) interrupts this appeal to objective evidence, but it is restored in verses 20 and 21 where the author seeks to impersonalize the process by which the prophecies of scripture came to be.

It should be noted that it is the origin, not the "interpretation" of prophecy, that the writer suggests derives solely from God. Barr apparently was not aware of this view.

According to the Eerdmans New Bible Commentary, the use of the word "interpretation" strains the Greek *epillusis* into an unnatural meaning. *Epillusis* speaks of origin not interpretation. The correct sense of the statement is that ultimately, no prophecy of scripture derives from any human source but has its origin in God.

Barr's observation (although he deals only with verses 20 and 21 and arrives at this point differently) that this passage of scripture points in a Catholic direction is therefore still valid.

The author's suggestion that the origin of prophecy is impersonal, is also a suggestion that its interpretation should not be left to any one person, that is, it is the province of the church (unfortunately in typically undemocratic mainstream practice this means only the clergy) not the individual member.

So here again a passage used by fundamentalists to support their understanding of scripture actually offers more support to the opposing Roman Catholic and mainstream view.

The reader should now be satisfied that the fundamentalists' assertion that their understanding of scripture is derived from scripture itself, is ill-founded.

It should be clear that the fundamentalist interpretation of the texts discussed above is just that; an interpretation. It is not the only interpretation possible, and more significantly, it is not the most accurate one.

The question must now be asked, if not scripture, what then is the true basis of the fundamentalists' approach to the Bible? This is the subject of the next chapter.

Chapter Three
The True basis of Fundamentalism

In the preceding chapter I made the point that the fundamentalist approach to the Bible is not a biblical one - at least not in the most informed sense of the word - because it is not based on proper biblical exegesis or interpretation.

Recognition of this fact is essential, if one is to overcome the terror of the Bible. That though is only one step in coming to an informed appreciation of the Bible and recognizing its beauty.

In this chapter, again using the literary-historical approach to biblical interpretation, which as I pointed out earlier, is a more holistic and rational approach than that which constitutes fundamentalism, I propose to show the reader that the true basis of the fundamentalist erroneous perception of the Bible is a series of historical factors, the first three of which listed below, heralded the very creation of the Bible and the institution we know as the church.

The identification of these fundamental factors as the true basis of the idyllic perception of scripture that I call the terror of the Bible therefore reaffirms my point that this unwholesome view of the Bible affects all Christendom.

The factors discussed are multidimensional and integrally related to each other. In the interest of brevity and simplicity, the following discussion does not seek to deal with them exhaustively and I have divided them under four headings: i) the influence of legalistic Judaism on the fledgling "Jesus movement" that constituted embryonic Christianity; ii) the introduction and establishment of the ekklesia; iii) the creation of a distinctly Christian canon, and iv) the error of the Reformers.

The reader should also bear in mind the psychological factor to which I referred earlier - that propensity of the human mind to seek to establish some infallible, unquestionable, unchanging authority around which we may order our perception of reality and regulate our conduct.

This is also a historical factor behind the terror of the Bible but it is not treated under a separate heading here because unlike the four others listed above, which are in the form of "events" (partly defined by chronological limits), this factor has the form of a condition.

What is more, this condition is not peculiar to fundamentalist Christians, nor even to religious persons on the whole. This perfectionist inclination is evident even among the irreligious. It is part of the human condition.

i) The influence of legalistic Judaism

One of the main historical factors behind the fundamentalist terror of the Bible is the influence of Judaism on the way the first Christians viewed scripture.

It is a very significant but much understated fact of church history that the first Christians were predominantly Jews. As Jews, these followers of the Nazarene[1] were prone to the legalistic preoccupation with scripture that characterized the Judaism of their day.

In Judaism, particularly of the post-exilic period (from about 587 BC on) God's will came increasingly to be seen as embodied in the very wording of the Jewish scriptures[2].

Several NT passages suggest that it was precisely against this legalistic, literalistic development that Jesus had reacted. For example, John 5:39 depicts Jesus as having referred to the scriptures in a rather sarcastic manner. This verse reads,

> Search the scriptures, for in them ye think ye have
> eternal life:

There is clearly a note of disapproval in this command; a note of disdain at the Jews' confidence in and reliance on their scriptures for eternal life. It is not a suggestion that the scriptures are useless but rather, that the Jews, in relying on them for eternal life, were expecting too much of them. The suggestion is that one should not rely on the scriptures for eternal life, but rather on Him of whom the scriptures testify ('and they are they which testify of me. ').

There is an appeal here for personal, experiential, if you will, spiritual knowledge, of Him in whom eternal life consists (consider John17:3).

In the preceding verse (John 5:38), Jesus had lamented the Jews' lack of such knowledge - their estrangement from the indwelling, individually, immediately or personally experienced word of God.

The incident recorded in this passage is not an isolated one. It is part of the overall emphasis on the "innate", non-legislative and spiritual nature of communion with God, that the author of the fourth gospel portrays Jesus as advocating (John 4:28; 3:5-8).

In John 6:44,45 we read,

> No man can come unto me, unless the father which
> hath sent me draw him:..It is written in the prophets, and
> they shall be all taught of God.
> Every man therefore that hath heard, and hath learned
> of the father, cometh unto me.

This is a reference to the mystical New Covenant as its advent was announced in Jeremiah 31:31-34. It is this unwritten New Covenant, not the written "New Testament", that Jesus is identified with in key passages (Malachi 3:1, Hebrews 8: 6-13; 12:14; also John 6: 44, 45).

It is difficult to imagine how in spite of such unambiguous teaching, followers of Jesus, even notoriously literalistic Jewish followers, could still be ensnared by the lure of legalism and literalism.

The inconsistency of the biblical material, particularly noticeable when one compares the spirituality of John's gospel with the emphasis on scripture in the gospel of Matthew (alluded to below, see page 85), does suggest that Jesus' rejection of Jewish legalism was not free of obscurity. This may explain his followers' subsequent resort to literalism.

However, that assessment hinges on the reliability of the biblical material itself. Modern biblical scholarship[3] obliges us not to overlook the possibility (some may say likelihood) that these records are not as representative of Jesus' words and deeds as is traditionally held.

It is conceivable therefore, that Jesus actually was more explicit in his denunciation of the Jews' attitude toward and interpretation of Torah: that is, that S. Westerholm's[4] suggestion that Jesus' teaching contained

> sufficient indications of a critical stance toward
> contemporary Torah observance to allow His adherents
> to abandon it.

is a gross understatement of the situation.

It is conceivable that Jesus did not only challenge and lower the popular Jewish estimate of their scriptures value sarcastically, but also, in very plain terms.

Take for example, this passage which appears in the apocryphal Gospel of the Nazarene[5] In a variant, but according to ISBE, plausible rendering of Matthew 18:15-22, the disciples ask Jesus how often they should forgive each other and he responds, seventy times seven,

> For in the prophets also...the sinful word was found.

If Jesus was this clear in his declaration of the limitations of scripture, the persistence of literalism among his followers may be more an indication of how deeply a literalistic approach to the scriptures was embedded in their thinking, than the result of his own equivocation or indecisiveness on the matter.

At any rate, virtually the same point is made if we do "blame" the obscurity of the biblical witness on Jesus himself.

If in spite of all his protestations against Jewish legalism, Jesus was still ambivalent in his attitude towards scripture, it only goes to show how deeply this preoccupation with the scriptures was embedded in his own subconscious mind.

This preoccupation would have proven the more formidable if, as some segments of biblical scholarship suggest, and I agree, Jesus saw his mission more as the reform of Judaism than the establishment of a new religion.

A distinction between different approaches to Judaism would imaginably not have been as obvious and easy to establish or maintain as a distinction between Judaism and an all-together different kind of religion.

However, the reader should bear in mind the following point which supports the view that Jesus was probably clear in his denunciation of legalism, or at least, that such denunciations were not unknown in his time.

It is known that in Jesus' day it was widely believed that the profoundest truth suffered if it was committed to writing.

Barr mentions[6] this fact of history, his point being the possibility that Jesus shared this unflattering view of the written word:

> it is quite possible that Jesus himself shared the common supposition in the cultural tradition of the time, namely that it was damaging to the profoundest truth if it was committed to writing. This is what Plato himself, on the Greek side, had believed; and on the Jewish side it was thought at the time that, although the Written Law by nature existed in scriptural form, the Oral Law which existed alongside it ought not to be committed to written form.

As to whether Jesus intended to start a new religion or merely to reform Judaism, it is also significant that the title "Christians" did not originate among Jesus' followers, but was imposed on them, probably insolently, by non-believers (Acts 11:26, 26:18; 1Peter 4:16). In the latter text, particularly, the Greek word *Chrestos*, translated "Christians", carries a pejorative connotation.

The precise nature of Jesus' mission as it relates to the terror of the Bible is discussed more fully in subsequent sections of this chapter. For now, I wish only to establish this; whether the cause of the "entrapment" of the first Christians in Jewish literalism lies with Jesus himself or his followers (or both), the one thing that is clear is the deep-seated nature of the legalism that he fought.

It was a historically entrenched tradition which, in spite of and beyond all that Jesus accomplished persisted into the mind-set of his followers.

It is an integral part of what Christianity has inherited from Judaism and a primary historical factor behind the terror of the Bible.

In chapter four I focus more fully on the propensity of all religions (not just Judaism or Christianity) to deteriorate into literalism.

ii) The introduction and establishment
   of the *ekklesia* in Christianity.

The next historical factor behind the terror of the Bible that we
shall be looking at here is the introduction and establishment of the
ekklesia in Christianity, that is, the conception of the body or
institution called the Church.

Here the establishment of the Church is viewed as the process
whereby leaders of the infant Christian movement founded this entity
in Jesus' name but apart from any historically credible suggestion that
Jesus himself intended to establish such a community or institution; it
is seen as that situation in which the centrality of the message of the
Kingdom of God in Jesus' preaching was obscured and or replaced by
the concept of the Church.

The creation of the Bible and its inordinate exaltation to the status
of an unquestionable authority - the terror of it - are held to be part of
the outcome of this process. Certainly, it is clear that the role and fate
of the Bible and the Church have always been inextricably linked.

In presenting this point of view, I shall be advancing a rather
unfamiliar picture of the Church's origins which I know may be
particularly inconceivable or unsettling to the average Christian.

This, more than anything else that I have shared so far, is the kind
of information that fundamentalists would label as "new doctrine" and
are most inclined to react suspiciously (or in paranoia) against.

I therefore feel obliged to point out that the most distinctive
characteristic of this kind of information is probably its current
accessibility, not its newness. It simply has not had a lot of publicity -
least of all among fundamentalists.

Most of this information has actually been around for some time. I
believe select interest groups (for example, translators of the many
ancient manuscripts in the Vatican library) have always had access to
this sort of information, but it has only become more easily accessible
since the simultaneous emergence of the literary-historical method of
biblical interpretation and the decline of dogmatism, paranoia and
prejudice among scholarly clerics.

Sadly, despite the accessibility of this information to the serious
inquirer, most fundamentalists have no inkling of the existence of this

data, far less of its reliability. In my case it was a matter of careful perusal of reference texts I had acquired at the local Christian Literature Crusade[1] book shop, and others stored in the library of the regional Anglican seminary Codrington College, located in Barbados.

At this point, I should also remind the reader that my reason for sharing this information is not to destroy the faith of Christians, but rather to show where that faith, because of a shallow historical content, is weak and harmful. Or, to put it more positively and precisely, my purpose is to impress upon those who embrace fundamentalist views, the need to strengthen and inform their faith: the need to make it more gracious, more conscientious and, ultimately, more beautiful.

I want to remind the reader that I am fully aware of how traumatic the process of informing one's faith can be. I know how painful it can be to discover that one's faith is not as well founded as one has been taught. Remember, I have personally experienced the uncertainty and anxiety that accompanies the dissolution of the "blessed assurance" of fundamentalist belief. I know how difficult it can be to have to re-orientate one's faith. I can only offer the reader the encouragement and comfort of my own experience; the assurance that the "end result" of this undertaking is well worth the discomfort that one suffers while engaged in the process.

Mind you, we never stop learning; one comes to certain points where one grasps the essence of the truth, but the process of working out the details seems infinite.

Nonetheless, this grasping of the essentials and being liberated thereby is worth the spiritual pain and uncertainty that one suffers while overcoming the terror of the Bible. It is the exact opposite of the shallow-fundamentalist, anti-intellectual and ultimately ill-founded exercise in which one is encouraged to believe the truth, but have little or no regard for knowing it. I alluded to this contradictory distinction between faith and knowledge in the introduction.

It is mentally unhealthy and can lead to profound confusion. I think it is significant that the author of the gospel according to John says you shall

KNOW the truth, and the truth shall make you free.

The reader is therefore challenged to read on courageously. Be confident, as I am, that nothing, including uncertainty about the Bible's reliability, can separate us from the love of God.

Again, if I have learned anything from my study of Christianity over the past seventeen years or so it is the integrity and legitimacy of doubting the Bible; that is, the legitimacy, even necessity, of recognizing that it contains contradictions, historical inaccuracies and other anomalies. As I stated earlier, it is only simplistic, ill-informed and superficial fundamentalism that insists on absolute certainty of the Bible's veracity.

More informed strains of Christianity recognize that[2]

> There are no infallible records anywhere; in the nature of the case, there cannot be, for we ourselves are far from infallible in understanding the record before us, and so were those who first composed them, compiled them, and transmitted them to posterity. It is asking too much - in fact, it is asking the impossible - to demand a clear, plain statement of "just what happened," or of "just what was said," without innuendo, overtone, allusion, or implicit reference of any kind. Only angels, not men, could understand such a record. We have this treasure "in earthen vessels" (2Cor. 4:7) - i.e., conditioned by all the limitations of human language, human understanding, the meaning of words, and especially the limits set to the unveiling of one person's inner consciousness to another. There are many questions we would like to ask, which can never be answered (Acts 1:6 ff). History, all history, is based on probabilities.

To speak of the infallibility of God's grace, as did Aquinas and others, is quite a different matter. To fully grasp the historical reality and beauty of that grace is truly revolutionary and worth any sacrifice, even a much loved, albeit erroneous perception of the Bible and the church.

Now, on with our discussion.

In the previous chapter, I noted that many scholars believe that Jesus' mission was to reform Judaism, not to start a new religion.

This opinion is strongly supported by the four gospels which indicate that the main theme of Jesus' preaching was the "Kingdom of God," in Greek, *he basileia tou theou*[1], not the church, Greek *ekklesia*.

References to the Kingdom are found throughout the gospels[3] but only the controversial gospel attributed to Matthew which is now recognized to be of a late origin (around A.D. 140), mentions the church - Matthew 16:18 and 18:17.

As IDB[4] points out, Jesus' concept of the Kingdom is not set out systematically or dogmatically anywhere in the Gospels, but the terms used imply that it was eschatological - the impending and final

> outward and visible manifestation of God's rule over the universe.

This eschatological or "end of time" phenomenon was the main theme of Jesus' parables (see endnote 10 of this chapter) and biblical scholarship is generally agreed that it is essentially different from what is signified by the Greek word *ekklesia*, that is, an assembly. At the very least, the *ekklessia*, is not presented as an eschatological phenomenon, that is, something reserved for the last days.

Yet historically, *ekklesia* has been viewed as a virtual synonym for the kingdom of God.

The fact is though, that in contrast to the obvious theological significance of the Greek *he basileia tou theou*, the Greek *ekklesia*, originating in secular Greek usage, denoted an assembly in the broadest, most commonplace and ordinary sense of the word[5].

In classical Greece *ekklesia* was a rather "neutral and colourless" term which was used indifferently, that is, "without basic shift in meaning" by believers and unbelievers alike.

Furthermore, *ekklesia* is essentially different in meaning from, and in its adaptability, contrasts with, the very word that has been used to translate it to English - the word "church".

"Church", a distinctly religious term, comes through German and Latin from the Greek word *kyriakos*, which means "that which belongs to the Lord" (note the similarity with the "Northern, espec Scot" Kirk). The idea of an assembly is not basic to this Greek term.

So we are faced with a rather surprising and complicated situation when we examine the origin of the key words *ekklesia* and "church" in Christian usage.

First, there is no substantive linguistic link between the concept of the kingdom of God and the term *ekklesia* which Christians have virtually made its synonym. Secondly, as IDB[6] so bluntly puts it,

> ...our English word "church" has no relation whatever to the Greek word Paul uses.

that is, *ekklesia*!

You get a sense of the extent of the discrepancy when you consider that even, the conservative Wycliffe Bible Encyclopedia[7] suggests that it is very unlikely that Jesus himself ever used the Greek term *ekklesia* because he spoke Aramaic, not Greek!

We shall discuss the apparent reference to the ekklesia by Jesus in Matthew's gospel shortly.

The question is, how and why did the *ekklesia* come to occupy such a critical and dominant role in Christianity, when informed biblical research suggests that it was virtually absent from Jesus' teachings?

The answer is to be found in the reinterpretation of Jesus' teaching by first century Christians.

IDB[8] acknowledges that those passages in the gospels which identify the kingdom with the church are not records of the words actually spoken by Jesus, but instead are

> ...late editorial revisions (especially in Matthew) which reflect the early christian point of view

Actually contemporary biblical scholarship has concluded that this type of reinterpretation, revision and, in many instances, embellishment (for example, the Angel at the pool of Bethesda story) is characteristic of the four gospels.

Commenting on the nature of the gospels IDB notes that,

> These are "theological" writings whose purpose is either to convince their contemporaries that Jesus is

divine and so to win them for eternal life (John 20: 30-31), or to set forth a more satisfactory interpretation of the meaning of his life than the one proposed by Jewish or pagan opponents or by Docetic Gnostics...

Our main concern here is with the Jewish opponents of Christianity because the reinterpretation of Jesus' teachings around the concept of the *ekklesia*, appears to have either caused, coincided with, or resulted from (they all seem plausible to me) the deep division and rivalry that arose between those Jews who believed that Jesus was the messiah and became his followers (Jewish-Christians), and those Jews who did not.

There is considerable evidence, both biblical and extra-biblical, that initially, Christianity was merely a sect within Judaism (like the Pharisees, and Essenes), but as it grew in the first century it met with rising opposition from the Jewish authorities which led to its establishment as an "independent" faith, sometime after A.D 70.

It was around A.D 70, following the destruction of the Temple at Jerusalem, that relations between Jesus' followers and other Jews plummeted to an all time low.

At that time, through what has been called the Council of Jamnia[9], the Jewish authorities introduced curses against the Christians in their synagogue prayers. This effectively made it impossible for those faithful to "the Nazerene" to attend synagogue worship (consider John 12:42).

Having been "flushed out" of the meetings of mainstream Judaism, Jewish Christians were therefore "forced" to hold their own meetings and in this context the introduction and centralization of the *ekklesia* occurred.

You see, the Christian and Jewish meetings followed very similar patterns (including the reading of the OT scriptures), so it has been suggested[10] that Christians adopted the title *ekklesia*, to counter any possible confusion of their meetings with the Jews' synagogue worship.

All of this occurred after Jesus' death (and resurrection?) and there is nothing in the Bible - properly understood in its historical context - which suggests that he intended or even foresaw it happening (note that Jesus himself taught in the synagogues: Matthew 4:23, 9:35,

13:54; Mark 1:39, 6:2; Luke 4:15,44; John 18:20).

This then, is the context in which the explicit record of Jesus as having declared his intention to establish an *ekklesia* in Matthew 16:18 is to be understood. This information by the gospel author is a retrospective editorial assumption: it is based on a presupposition of Jesus' intention to establish a new religion; his own *ekklesia*.

The reader may also benefit from a consideration of IDB's discussion of the gospel writers' presupposition of Jesus' "messianic consciousness", (Jesus Christ, A. 2. h. The question of authenticity).

Let me say here that I think it is rather odd that while recognizing the inclusion and centrality of such presuppositions in the gospels, IDB could still refer to these writings as,

> ...the historical part - of the early Christian Kerygma, the
> proclamation of the message of salvation...

I find it hard to see how any record, in which such *presuppositions* (not probabilities) are so prominent, could be viewed as historical.

IDB does offer some justification of this view, where it is noted that "our modern types of history and biography did not exist in the ancient world. "

Still, while I am no authority on the ancient concepts of history and biography, I do not think they could have been so akin to that of myth, or else, so unlike our own, as to allow blithe acceptance of known exaggerations or falsifications.

And even if they were, I do not believe that in this modern age, we are obliged or, in our best interest advised, to embrace or condone such concepts of history and biography.

Furthermore, while I may agree tentatively with the IDB commentators, that

> ...the motive which led to the reinterpretation and
> reformulation of some of Jesus' sayings, in the interest of
> making clear his own awareness of the supreme role he
> was to play in the purposes of God, was a perfectly
> natural one

I most strongly reject the proposition that it was an "inevitable" one.

That conclusion is based on the assumption that the "New Testament" writers and compilers had no questions about Jesus' self-consciousness, and implies that they had no choice but to interpret his sayings as they did: that is, essentially, endowing him with a "messianic consciousness" and making the concepts of the Kingdom and the *ekklesia* synonymous.

Coming from one of the more progressive quarters of contemporary biblical scholarship, I think such a conclusion is sadly conservative and retrogressively traditional, and it ignores or severely minimizes important evidence which points to other possible conclusions. Evidence such as IDB itself outlines, that Jesus never claimed to be the messiah and evidence of the disparity between the concepts of the Kingdom and the *ekklesia*.

This IDB conclusion, in my opinion, seems to be a classic example of the outworking of that self-preserving impulse I spoke of in chapter one: that idealistic, defensive impulse which militates against acknowledgment and or acceptance of the anomalies, irregularities and shortcomings that are at the root of traditional Christianity; that impulse which, in the face of modern biblical criticism, resorts to a fundamentalist naiveté and so promotes that perfectionistic, intimidating view of the Bible which makes it a terror.

This book is dedicated to the extinction of that primitive impulse. As I see it, the right response to the challenges of modern biblical criticism - the way forward - entails the courageous acknowledgment of the true conception of the Church and the determination of its mission in modern times accordingly.

Our main priority must be to ascertain the *truth* about the Bible and the Church, not to maintain traditional views about them. We must see that by failing or refusing to pursue the truth, we do the greatest dishonour to the Bible, the Church and the life, mission and memory of Jesus of Nazareth.

And so, in accordance with the findings of objective, literary-historical biblical analysis I am urging that it be recognized by Christians everywhere that the conception of the Church was not intended or foreseen by Jesus.

Jesus' main theme was the Kingdom of God, and while his proposed establishment of this Kingdom by spiritual means, rather than physical force, may have been novel in Judaism (Zechariah 4:6

which says "not by might" being a possible indication to the contrary), the idea of the Kingdom itself was not unfamiliar and probably imposed nothing new on the basic composition or structure of Judaism, nor warrant a break with that religion.

This cannot be said for the *ekklesia*.

The *ekklesia* presented in the Bible appears as the religious opposite of the Jews' synagogue: the two are not compatible. Indeed, they tend to be mutually exclusive historically.

In its conception the church was apparently intended to be the antithesis of the synagogue. This was probably the thinking behind the biblical reference to the Jewish assembly as "the synagogue of Satan" (Revelation 2:9 and 3:9), an unfortunate reference that has no doubt fuelled anti-Jewish sentiment over the centuries.

Now, I am not suggesting that the break between Judaism and its Christian sect led inevitably to the terror of the Bible. Had the break been "grounded" differently, that is, had the new religion (Christianity) been established more firmly and prominently on the principle of the internally-oriented New Covenant, instead of the externally-oriented *ekklesia*, the terror of the Bible could possibly have been precluded.

The point I am making is that the importance of the Bible was overrated because the new religion was externally-oriented, focusing on public notions of morality and spirituality - as it still is today - and so relied on the Bible for validation and control.

Put differently, the introduction and establishment of the externally-oriented (public) *ekklesia* as the object and focus of Jesus' mission precipitated the establishment of an externally-oriented (public) standard by which it could be regulated.

The Bible, alone or in conjunction with other implements of outer-tradition (rituals like Baptism, Communion, vestments etc, and church "officers", pastors, deacons, evangelists, the pope, and so on) became that standard.

Simultaneously, the significance of the internally-oriented (private, heart-centred) New Covenant was obscured, and the stage was set for the development of the terror of the Bible.

However, and I have shown the support for this view within the scriptures, Jesus was not calling for a new or improved literary canon or standard. He was calling for a different attitude toward the one (the

Jewish scriptures) that already existed. He was urging the recognition of scripture's limitations - the limitations of all written matter as a means of communicating the will of God.

He was not distinguishing between two written codes. He was emphasizing the difference between one that is written and one that is not. The first Christians, or else their immediate successors, apparently never really grasped this.

Now, the question arises as to how the heart-oriented concept of the New Covenant can be reconciled to the preaching of the Kingdom, which the four gospels suggest was Jesus' main theme, and which was obviously represented as an external phenomenon - something which would ultimately be clearly visible to all humanity (Matthew 24:27, Mark 13:26, Luke 17:24).

In the past I would have drawn the reader's attention to Luke 17:21 which declares that the Kingdom is "in you" but my scholarly sources have informed me that this passage is misleading. IDB and other authorities suggest that the reference here is not to that which is "in" us, but rather, to that which is "among" us. This interpretation suggests that the Kingdom, like the *ekklesia* is externally oriented.

Granted that this may be so (it is not necessarily[11]), I do not think it minimizes or contradicts the innateness and individualism, that is, the element of individual autonomy and mysticism that characterizes Jesus' preaching in the gospels (especially in the gospel according to John, e.g. 3:8 "the wind blows where it listeth") and is the essence of the concept of the New Covenant.

This is because the external dimension of the Kingdom of God is not its primary focus. The primary focus of, or operative word in the phrase "kingdom of God", is God; the emphasis is on *whose* the kingdom is, not on how it is constituted, e.g. whether it is an individualistic or group phenomenon.

So then, while the external element in the concept of the Kingdom of God is obvious, it is not inconsistent with, nor does it preclude an innate, individualistic dimension.

Emphasis on the concept of the kingdom, whether in reference to its external (public) or internal (private) dimensions, or indeed to both, is in fact consistent with emphasis on the concept of the New Covenant.

This however is not the case with the term *ekklesia*. *Ekklesia* always refers to a group, an assembly. The only variation in the biblical use of *ekklesia* is that it sometimes designates a local group (Matthew 18:17, Romans 16:1, 3-5, 1Corinthians 1:2) and other times it refers to the universal body of Christians (Matthew 16:18, 1Timothy 3:15).

Ekklesia never identifies an individualistic or private reality: it is always public: it is an externally oriented term.

Emphasis on the concept of the *ekklesia* is therefore fundamentally at odds with the propagation of the heart-oriented, privacy-centred New Covenant. Indeed, the traditional propagation of the *ekklesia* inevitably undermines the innate, private or mystical focus of the teachings of Jesus of Nazareth.

I am prepared to say that the *ekklesia* has only been associated with Jesus because it has arisen out of the very religious milieu which revolved around his propagation of the New Covenant and, more than this, because its advocates (the more questionable and rapacious of whom I unapologetically call *ekklesiasticks*) purport to endorse the principle of the New Covenant - the principle of individual autonomy.

It is largely because of this allegiance to the concept of the New Covenant - albeit rather superficial - that the *ekklesia* has survived its unnatural birth, and continues to survive to this day as a force to be reckoned with.

The same individualistic component in Christianity is what made the sixteenth century Reformation inevitable, and also, guaranteed its relative[12] success.

It is also behind the persistence of liberal Protestantism and, ironically, it is to a large extent responsible for the phenomenal growth, since 1906, of the ardently fundamentalist Pentecostal movement.

One of the great boasts of Pentecostal Christians against the traditional churches and persons who embrace other religions generally, is that Christianity is not a religion, but rather a relationship - a personal relationship with Jesus.

I certainly heard that a lot among my Pentecostal peers, and claimed it too, while I was content to carry the label Pentecostal. My confident assurance was (and, incidentally, still is) that God's Spirit was bearing witness with my spirit (Romans 8:16).

This is what the New Covenant is all about, and it is this emphasis on the role of the Spirit in the life of the individual, that is behind the spontaneity and vitality of Pentecostalism and its consequent growth and appeal today.

Unfortunately, the liberating individualism of Pentecostalism is bound to the ecclesiastical constraints of that movement - its "groupisms" or public-oriented traditions (Yes. Pentecostals have traditions too.), with which all its adherents are expected to comply.

Pentecostals are no more immune to an emphasis on conformity than any of the other church groups; conformity is essential to the idea of the *ekklesia*.

Now don't misunderstand me. I am not knocking conformity per se. Some degree of conformity is necessary, and inevitable if human interaction (society) is to flourish. I am not advocating indifference to the interests and preferences of others. I am not suggesting that churches should be done away with - as if that were possible.

What I am saying is that groups and institutions advocating conformity must have greater regard to individual freedom. There must be balance. The individualistic New Covenant principle must be recognized and respected.

I am not saying that Christians should forsake the assembling of themselves together, but rather, that they should not "come together" in a manner which fosters divisions among themselves, and or prejudice against the rest of the world. In their coming together they must recognize that everyone in this world is essentially *together* - that is, we all constitute humanity, in spite of our several individual views.

Interestingly, our individuality ('oneness') is the basis of our humanity. We all share it, and are consequently interdependent.

Social codes and constitutions are important and inevitable if society is to function relatively smoothly. However, such regulation is least effective when it is advocated or imposed without regard to the rights and interests of the individual.

There must be tolerance, there must be compromise, especially in religious matters - matters that are essentially to do with that which is invisible: matters of the heart.

There will always be conflict and tension between private and public morality. If we are wise we will try to minimize (note that I did not say "trivialize") this conflict and try to keep the tensions at a minimum.

I believe this tolerance is precisely what Jesus was trying to teach his generation. I believe the conception of the *ekklesia* was an error to the extent that it ignored, undermined or simply just missed the point of this teaching.

Something very similar has occurred in virtually all other religions that have been around for any considerable length of time. A simple but profound truth or principle is expressed, is recorded or re-enacted for the benefit of posterity, and with the passage of time that truth or principle becomes encased in a series of increasingly more elaborate records or re-enactments, until finally the essential truth itself is lost sight of or obscured, and its commemoration becomes an empty, or mostly impotent ritual (see the article TRADITION in ISBE).

Another relatively progressive fundamentalist publication, The World's Religions[13], refers to this process and/or its outcome as "priestcraft".

In Christianity, priestcraft is manifested in the perennial problem of religious exploitation and oppression.

The Church will probably never overcome this problem entirely, but its leaders can at least set the stage for priestcraft to be dealt with more effectively by attacking it at its root, namely the Church's own anomalous conception; the conception of the *ekklesia*.

As I stated earlier, the Church must come to terms with the truth of its origins. Any loss, embarrassment or injury which Christianity suffers in this quest is far outweighed by the benefits that stand to be gained - paramount among which, is the eradication of the terror of the Bible and a deeper and fuller appreciation of its beauty.

There is much at stake here. The extent to which we fail to cultivate a sound, balanced understanding of the conception of the *ekklesia* - recognizing not only the good but also the evil that is at its roots - is the extent to which we make provision for the perpetuation of beliefs and views that undermine the good that it accomplishes today and may accomplish in the future.

The words of C.S. Lewis (front cover) regarding Christianity's confession of its contribution to "the sum of human cruelty and treachery" comes to mind here[14].

If ever the book which I am not going to write is

85

written it must be the full confession by Christendom of Christendom's specific contribution to the sum of human cruelty and treachery. Large areas of "the World" will not hear us till we have publicly disowned much of our past. Why should they? We have shouted the name of Christ and enacted the service of Moloch.

We now move on to the discussion of another important historical factor behind Christianity's terror of the Bible - another stage in the establishment of the church. The creation of the Christian canon.

iii) The creation of a distinctly Christian canon

Another significant historical factor behind the terror of the Bible is the creation of a distinctly Christian canon - that canon which itself came to be known as the Bible.

At first glance, it may seem that I am merely stating the obvious, that is, that there could be no "terror of the Bible" if the Bible had not been created. However, my point here goes deeper than that. I hope to show - more explicitly than I may have so far - that the creation of a literary canon was fundamentally incompatible with the preaching and mission of Jesus Christ.

The word "canon" is of Christian origin, from the Greek *kanon*, which is derived from a Semitic root borrowed from the Sumerian *gina*, which means "reed" or "cane".

From this came the idea first of a measuring rod, later a rule or norm of faith, and last of all, and most unnaturally, a catalogue or list.

The term *kanon*, translated "rule", appears in Galations 6:16 and Philippians 3:16, where it signifies a principle or pattern. *Kanon* was first employed of the books of scripture in the technical sense of a standard collection of sacred writings by the church-fathers of the 4th Century (ISBE)[1].

The first distinctly Christian canon, or list of texts, was introduced by Marcion who was born in Sinope, Pontus (Asia Minor), the son of the bishop.

Marcion arrived in Rome around AD 140 and embraced the teachings of the gnostic Cerdo who believed that the God of the

Jewish scriptures (the "Old Testament") was not the God and father of Jesus. Cerdo contended that the God of the Jewish scriptures was unknowable, whereas Jesus had revealed his father; that Judaism's God was basically vengeful, a God of sheer justice, driven by anger to order battles and slaughter, whereas Jesus' God was loving, gracious and merciful.

Marcion became the chief advocate of this message and added his own distinctive ideas.

In accordance with his rejection of the "Old Testament" or Jewish scriptures as the product of a God inferior to the Christian God, Marcion established a distinctively "Christian" canon - the very first canon of exclusively Christian scriptures that we know of.

Marcion's canon was "hyper-Paulinistic", that is, it was based and focused predominantly on the work of Paul, and consisted of two parts, "gospel" and "apostle" (Gk. *evangeline* and *apostolos*). He included Luke's gospel - the sole gospel included in this canon - because of Luke's association with Paul; the apostolic section was limited to ten Pauline Epistles (the Pastorals are missing). Marcion purged from Luke any passages incompatible with his own doctrine and in the apostolic section he gave Galations prominence because of its anti-Judaizing thrust.

The creation of this canon is Marcion's most crucial contribution to Christianity and a primary historical factor behind the fundamentalist terror of the Bible. You see, without a Christian Bible - an authoritative body of writings distinct from that of the Jews - there would arguably be no terror of the Bible in Christianity.

Now, Marcion's canon is hardly known today but that is only because it was not embraced by that segment of Christian opinion which subsequently dominated the *ekklesia* - those Christians who felt it was beneficial or necessary to maintain a scriptural link with Judaism.

These persons may well have been mostly of Jewish origin and consequently found the rejection of the Jewish scriptures and the break with Judaism that Marcion advocated unacceptable.

It may also have been a matter of political and or economic "expediency". As with many new movements, there were probably persons in the young Jesus movement who did not want to provoke opposition from any quarter and at the same time welcomed whatever funding, goodwill or other support they could get within Judaism. There is nothing intrinsically improper in such motives.

For whatever reason (I think a combination of the above is most likely), the rejection of the Jewish scriptures that Marcion advocated was unacceptable to these Christians.

Yet, they saw the wisdom of having a literary, Christian canon of their own. The introduction of Marcion's canon had resulted in the expansion of his following; according to the ISBE article cited above[2] "Marcionitic churches had sprang up in alarming numbers" following the introduction of his canon. His detractors' solution to this dilemma was the creation of their own canon, the Christian canon with which we are most familiar - that canon which combines both the Jewish and Christian scriptures.

This undertaking was largely aided by the error of Tertullian, another prominent churchman who I mentioned earlier. You will recall that it was Tertullian who first referred to Christian writings as the "New Testament" (Latin *Novum Testamentum*) and thereby initiated the confusion of those writings with the mystical New Covenant, and the virtual substitution of the former for the latter.

At the time of his error, Tertullian was not responding to Marcion's challenge though; he was responding to the alleged "threat" of the Montanists.

This group of Christians had arisen in Asia minor around A.D 172 when a young convert named Montanus rose to prominence as a prophet.

Montanists claimed to be mouthpieces of the *paraclete*, the Greek title given to the Holy Spirit in John's gospel. They distinguished themselves as persons who "spoke from God", in the first person pronoun, as the Old Testament prophets were reported to have done (2Peter 1:21), and they called their own prophecies "New Prophecy" - corresponding with the New Covenant.

The Montanists' claim of divine inspiration for their sayings amounted to an equation of themselves with the first apostles and indeed, with Jesus himself (which, by the way would probably not have been as big, an issue if Jesus was viewed as a Jewish reformer, rather than the founder of a new faith).

Tertullian and others, who were just then promoting their own literary canon against Marcion's found this unacceptable because, like

Marcion, the Montanists claims challenged and undermined the authority (based on an exclusive concept of divine inspiration) that they were reserving for their own canon.

The "threat" of the Montanists' New Prophecy was apparently averted therefore, by the identification of the Christian scriptures as the "New Testament".

Now, in commenting on Marcion's role in the creation of the "New Testament" canon, ISBE observes that many scholars, and especially Adolf von Harnack are of the opinion that it was in conscious reaction to Marcion's canon that the church-fathers established the basic dimensions of the present canon. The author of this ISBE article then challenges Harnack's opinion and suggests that the church-fathers would have established a distinctly Christian literary canon without Marcion's prompting.

This, in my view, demonstrates and underscores the seriousness of the problem I am addressing here. In his preoccupation with who gets *credit* for the introduction of the "New Testament" canon or whether or not the introduction of this canon is seen as reactionary, the author of the article is clearly oblivious to the fact that the introduction of this canon signaled the church-fathers' fundamental, decisive departure from the anti-literalistic teachings of Jesus!

The author's willingness to commend the creators of the "New Testament" canon shows absolutely no consciousness of the fact that the creation of this canon - indeed the entire Christian canon - represents the undermining of the critical distinction (evident in these very same "New Testament" scriptures, e.g. Romans 2:29 and 2Corinthians 3:6-17), between the letter (Jewish Old Covenant writings) and the Spirit (the New Covenant principle).

The article clearly demonstrates that for approximately two thousand years, some of the most prominent scholars professing to be Jesus' disciples have failed to grasp this basic and critical point of his teachings: in the determination of righteousness, the invisible etchings on people's hearts are of greater importance than what is written visibly.

They have failed to comprehend the nature and significance of the New Covenant.

This failure has cost Christianity greatly. A literal Christian canon - Marcion's or anyone else's - is no substitute for the New Covenant.

Now, I am not without sympathy for the literary canonists. They were living in a difficult time for Christians.

Apart from all the challenges Christians faced externally, there was internal wrangling as rival groups competed for the loyalty of the masses to their various interpretations of Jesus' teachings - much like today.

You see, the death of the apostles had created a power vacuum - an authority crisis. ISBE puts it this way:

> ...the death of the apostles posed a new question, one that received different answers, or at least an ambivalent answer, in the age of the fathers. The question was an obvious one: What is the locus of apostolic authority after the passing of the apostles themselves?...On who or what does authorization come in succession to the apostles?

A literary canon probably did seem a very attractive and effective means of filling this vacuum; a means of achieving unity (or at least uniformity) and ensuring the preservation and expansion of the church.

After all, it had worked for Marcion. As is noted earlier, the number of his followers increased substantially after he introduced his canon.

Nonetheless, as is abundantly clear today, neither Marcion's nor any of the other Christian canons that were introduced subsequently (the Mormons' which includes the writings of Joseph Smith is a fairly recent example) have brought any enduring, truly meaningful resolution to the wrangling that has plagued Christianity from its inception.

Indeed, the introduction of the Christian Bible (the establishment of a scriptural canon in Christianity) has instead largely served to consolidate differences of opinion among Christians.

It has instead facilitated greater intransigence, prejudice, and hysteria. It has been exploited by competing groups and individuals within Christendom, each claiming it as the basis of their "objectivity" and authority.

The situation could not be otherwise. The canonization of

scripture - which is actually the establishment of scripture as an unquestionable standard or measurement of righteousness - encourages literalism, and literalism breeds disunity.

The example of the Jewish "canon" - and I use the term loosely here since the Jews' concept of canonicity seems to have been less rigid than the church's[3] - should have convinced Christians of this. Indeed, as I have already stated, that was the focal point of Jesus' apparent attempt to reform Judaism.

It is important that I reemphasize the point, made in the first chapter, that it was the church-fathers who committed the error of introducing and establishing a literary canon in Christianity.

I do so because it seems that some authorities in the older traditional or mainstream churches would have us believe that Christians' preoccupation with scripture began with modern day fundamentalists or their predecessors of the Reformation era.

Virtually the same opinion has been expressed by an acquaintance of mine, who is a prominent scholarly priest in the Anglican church in the Caribbean.

It is true that the church-fathers subscribed in large measure to the doctrine of apostolic succession and so posited divine authority in the descendants of Jesus' first disciples - obviously, eventually including themselves.

However it would be rash and erroneous to conclude that this was their only, or even primary, basis of authority. As the ISBE quotation above indicates, the question of authority in the church has been a point of contention from the Church's inception, with scripture and the human mediators of Christ's authority being cited as the final arbiter alternately and together, at various times.

What is more, despite Christians' historical "playing" of the Church (that is, its officers) against scripture and vice versa it would appear that overall the two mediums tend to be mutually validating and sustaining (justifying).

This is a point I have made repeatedly. In chapter two I also made the point that I do not favour either of these two "media" as the ultimate ground of faith[4]. However, my focus right now is on the inappropriateness, indeed, the inability of scripture to fill this role.

And so, I submit that instead of elevating a scriptural canon to the status of an unquestionable authority, the Church-Fathers should have acknowledged and given prominence to the ultimate authority of the mystical New Covenant - not confuse this heart oriented phenomenon with a literary canon.

Now, I am not suggesting that elevating the New Covenant would have put an end to all differences of opinion among Christians. I do not think Christians will ever agree on all aspects of their faith. However, it is possible to "agree to disagree". In other words, the problem is not our differing opinions, but rather our attitudes toward our differing opinions.

Acknowledgment of the reality and validity of the radically individualistic New Covenant phenomenon entails recognition of the inevitability and validity of differing opinions and so engenders a conciliatory attitude toward persons whose views differ from our own.

It is because the privacy-oriented New Covenant is not being acknowledged that some of us, most conspicuously fundamentalists, are so inflexible and uncompromising; so narrow-minded and one-sided in our faith. We are not trying hard enough to appreciate others' points of view. We succumb and subscribe to that ungracious, literalistic and legalistic concept of God which Jesus saw in Judaism and opposed.

Furthermore, like Marcion who opposed this religious arrogance and divisiveness in Judaism, but yet became ensnared by it himself, our concept of God is too restrictive; too idealistic and unforgiving (Marcion failed to forgive those Jews who rejected Jesus).

This unwholesome concept of God, which is born of fear and begets a self-preserving and self-righteous attitude is a part of both the root and the fruit of the literalistic terror of the Bible.

The development of the concept of heresy, which THC[5] identifies as a key factor by which "...Christianity began to acquire a recognizable shape and a sense of identity..." demonstrates how this attitude may be instituted in a religion.

Originally the Greek word *hairesis*, translated "heresy" merely signified a choice or opinion.

It was only as followers of Jesus started to externally standardize (remember, the New Covenant focuses primarily on internal standards) his teachings, only as the requirement for "faith" gave way to the need to embrace "the faith", and as conviction was obscured by creed, and Christianity became more institutionalized and less personal, that *hairesis* took on its current technical, negative connotation[6] of a "damnable opinion".

This development was in fact concurrent with the canonization of the Christian writings and signaled the emergence of an intolerance in Christianity that has plagued the church ever since.

It is the development of that unhealthy, intimidating concept of God and intolerant attitude toward others that is manifest in the terror of the Bible. Had the New Covenant been given the prominence in Christianity which it deserves - the prominence which I believe Jesus intended it to have - that concept of God and attitude toward each other would probably have been averted.

Next we consider the error of the Reformers.

iv) The error of the Reformers

We now come to the fourth and final historical factor behind the terror of the Bible that I shall be discussing; the error of the Reformers.

I have included the following perspective on the sixteenth century Reformation here because I believe that in spite of the democratic gains that were made in Christianity during the Reformation, this era nonetheless represents a point at which the idealized authority, and hence the terror of the Bible, was reinforced.

The Reformation is generally seen as a positive development in Christianity - a time of liberation from the corruption and restrictiveness that characterized the medieval church. This view is largely justifiable.

However, the Reformers made a fundamental error when they decided that the Bible was an "innocent" or rather, flawless, tool of manipulation in the hands of corrupt church-leaders.

They apparently assumed that the degeneration that had overtaken the church was solely the result of the church's allegorical interpretation and misrepresentation of the Bible's teachings. They evidently believed that this alone had given rise to the unchallenged power and authority of the church and its consequent corruption.

While obviously having a lot of merit, this analysis of the situation was too simplistic.

93

The Reformers were not mindful of the fact that the allegorical interpretation of the Bible arose from - or at least was justified in the minds of Christians - by the church's belief that the Bible as a divinely inspired document, was intrinsically accurate and true; in other words, that it was "inerrant and infallible".

The Reformers did not realize, perhaps could not, that it was this idealistic perception of the Bible which precipitated its allegorical interpretation and in turn led to the excessive power of the Church and its consequent corruption - absolute power corrupts absolutely.

The fact is, the Reformers' concept of the Bible's "inspiration" was virtually identical to that which empowered and was being exploited by the Roman Catholic Church.

Like their Catholic predecessors, the Reformers embraced an idealistic view of scripture's "inspiration" in which the human element was totally obscured under traditional (especially Judaism's) presuppositions about the divine influence and effect.

Consequently, when the Reformers replaced the absolute authority of the Pope (speaking ex cathedra through church councils etc.) with the absolute authority of the Bible, they merely reinforced and crystallized the erroneous and intimidating perception of the Bible that had empowered the Catholic church.

In so doing, the Reformers simply set the stage for the replacement of one form of biblical exploitation by another - their own. The Reformers failure to deal with the core of the exploitation, namely, the Church's access to absolute power through its "creation" of an infallible tool (the Bible), ultimately led to their own contribution to this problem.

The abuses of self-centred Popes which the reformers so zealously protested, have long been duplicated, and in some instances possibly exceeded, by self-serving and deluded Protestant priests and pastors (puny pontiffs) who use the Bible to impose their will upon others.

In principle, there is no difference between the sale of indulgences by the medieval church and the insistence of many contemporary Protestants that it is a sin (robbery) not to give a tenth (tithe) of one's earnings "to God", via the church. Please note that I am not knocking the perfectly acceptable practice of requesting wholly voluntary financial support for your church's programs, when done in a context of transparency and mutual accountability of clergy and laity.

94

Continuing: even Luther, that champion of the Protestant Reformation who exposed the vagaries of the ancient and medieval church's elaborate fourfold[1] scheme of allegorical biblical interpretation and insisted on adherence to the "plain meaning" of the text was not above reproach in his use of the Bible.

In his zeal to promote the Protestant cause, his claim that his best skill was only "..to give the literal, simple sense of scripture.." proved somewhat shallow.

This point is made in ISBE's article on the history of biblical interpretation[2].

> Unfortunately, however, Luther did not grant the literary-historical method exclusive rights in the interpretation of scripture. He once quoted Paul's warning in 1 Cor. 3:10ff that others should be careful to build upon the foundation of Jesus Christ, and commented ' All this is spoken of the ministry, so that he who would treat scripture and explain it well may be sure so to treat it as to teach nothing but what agrees with the doctrine of faith, which alone stands firm and is founded on Christ" (WA, XXIV, 549). Luther never explained why his understanding of justification by faith alone was the "doctrine of faith" by which all the Bible should be interpreted. Some parts of scripture fared badly as Luther applied his rule to them.

This prominent Reformer is notorious for his reference to St. James' epistle as "an epistle of straw" because of its denunciation of "faith without works".

ISBE also notes the Protestant John Calvin's inconsistency in interpreting the Bible, pointing out that he too is known to have set certain books of the "New Testament" above others.

In essence, and ironically, the Reformers replaced the medieval Roman church's exploitation of scripture which was based on emphasis on the Bible's obscurity and allegorical interpretation, with their own brand of exploitation, based on claims of the Bible's perspicuity – the clearness of its teaching.

This exploitation of the Bible by the first Protestants was ironic but it was also inevitable, because they had inherited the Catholic church's access to absolute power. Indeed, they did not merely allow the Catholic church's idealistic perception of the Bible to remain intact, they actually strengthened it.

Barr notes that in spite of all its novelty, emerging Protestant theology was marked by the wholesale importation of important segments of Catholic dogma[3].

Amazingly, the doctrine of scripture that the Reformers developed - the focal point of the reform they established - was fundamentally in harmony with Roman Catholic teaching.

Like their Catholic predecessors, the Reformers failed to see that the Bible was no more infallible than the men who wrote and compiled it. They were probably too much the victims of the idealistic and intimidating terror of the Bible themselves, to recognize their dilemma and error.

Ultimately, Protestants were no more willing or able to relinquish the medieval Roman church's unhealthy doctrine of "inspiration" than they were to accept its method of interpretation or its doctrine of papal infallibility.

They denounced the Roman Church's allegorical approach to Biblical interpretation but held on to the basic understanding of scripture that is the root (and fruit, in as much as it is a self-perpetuating concept) of that approach.

Let me say again that it is not my intention to minimize the gains that were made in Christianity through the efforts of Luther, Calvin and other Protestant leaders.

They rid Christianity of Roman Catholic domination, in large measure, and reintroduced a heritage of free thought and free inquiry - the integrity and validity of individual faith - which, in spite of all its hazards (real or imagined), appears to have been a basic tenet of Jesus' teachings and is indispensable to the soundness of Christian faith and a well grounded appreciation of the Bible's beauty.

Nonetheless, the point must be made, that by hinging the validity of individual faith on virtually the same erroneous perception of scripture as the Catholic Church's, the Reformers devalued and undermined the very individualism that spawned their movement.

Significant change has only come about since the emergence of Liberal Protestantism. This branch of Christianity, mentioned in the preceding chapter, has exposed the defective basis of the sola scriptura battle cry of Protestant profession.

It is my hope that fundamentalists whom so readily identify with the Reformers, and all others who commend their efforts, will realize the basic kinship or unity of their understanding of the Bible with that of medieval Roman Catholicism.

The error of the Reformers must be recognized, if Christianity is to be rid of the terror of the Bible or that "terror" is to be minimized.

I have now completed my discussion of those historical factors which I see as the true basis of the fundamentalist terror of the Bible. The following is a summary of the main points.

First of all, I highlighted the influence of legalistic Judaism on Christianity. I noted that many of the early Christians, being Jews and having their faith tied to, controlled and dominated by a legalistic preoccupation with scripture, were naturally inclined to transfer this legalism onto the writings of the Church.

Essentially, I sought to show that the tendency toward legalism is an integral part of what all Christians have inherited from Judaism and a significant historical factor behind the terror of the Bible.

Next I treated the very conception of the church as an essentially error-plagued or ill-conceived undertaking which has precipitated the terror of the Bible. Accordingly, I elaborated on the argument, taken up in the previous section, that Jesus' mission was to reform Judaism, not to start a new religion. I noted that Jesus' main theme was the Kingdom of God, not the *ekklesia*, that is the Church.

Furthermore, I brought to the reader's attention documented evidence which suggests that the idea of the *ekklesia* was first introduced among Christians as a response to their expulsion from the Jewish synagogue, following the council of Jamnia.

I went on in section ii of this chapter to show that while the concept of the Kingdom of God is consistent with that of the New Covenant, which also featured prominently in Jesus' teaching, the concept of the *ekklesia* is not.

Ultimately, I sought to make it clear to the reader that the externally oriented concept of the *ekklesia* is fundamentally at odds with, and in fact undermines Jesus' emphasis on the internally oriented, mystical New Covenant.

In section iii I focused on the introduction of the Christian canon and asserted the point that the creation of a literary canon was fundamentally incompatible with the preaching and mission of Jesus Christ.

Here I once again had the support of documented evidence. This time the evidence showed that the creation of the first literary Christian canon by Marcion, was ill-conceived, like the establishment of the *ekklesia*. I pointed out the undisputed fact that Marcion's canon, was an unwise and ill-fated response to the challenge of Judaism.

I also made the point - to which I imagine there will be opposition - that the creation of our present canon (which combines the Jewish and Christian writings) was equally unwise and no real improvement on Marcion's canon, at least in so far as a literary canon was not the answer to the divisiveness and disorder that characterized infant Christianity.

My contention is that the answer was (and still is) a fuller understanding and promotion of the New Covenant phenomenon - a fuller recognition of the final authority of conscience.

Finally, while conceding that significant gains were made during the Reformation, I addressed the error of the Reformers.

I suggested that Luther and his counterparts failed to see the true source of the church's corruption, and so, unwittingly compounded the problem. I argued that the Reformers did not realize that the Roman church's perception of scripture, which they themselves embraced, was idyllic and unsound - virtually giving any individual or group who controlled the Bible access to absolute power and authority and thus inducing exploitation.

Again using documented evidence, I showed how the Reformers, (particularly Luther and Calvin) having reinforced the church's idyllic view of scripture, proceeded to manipulate and exploit the Bible themselves.

In closing this chapter I think I can safely say that having outlined the true basis of the fundamentalist terror of the Bible, which is the historical factors behind this long-lived phenomenon, I have at least challenged the idea that the Bible was meant to be: that is, I have challenged the idea that its existence was planned by God.

I have at least challenged the idea,

... that christianity was supposed to be a scripturally
controlled religion in the same way as the Judaism of
Jesus' time was a scripturally controlled religion.

to use Barr's words[4].

Beyond this, I have also demonstrated the point, made from the outset of this book, that the intimidating perception of the Bible that is being addressed here should not be blamed solely on the typically fundamentalist churches (Pentecostals, Baptists, Seventh Day Adventists etc) but rather that we must recognize the role of the older traditional churches (Catholics, Anglicans etc) in the creation and perpetuation of this problem.

If we grasp the nature and extent of the problem before us, we will realize that it has its roots in the very conception of the Bible and the church. We will also realize that any meaningful solution to the problem must entail a radical re-evaluation of Christianity.

Hopefully, this will lead to a more enlightened attitude toward scripture - an attitude that brings our understanding of scripture into harmony with a greater understanding and appreciation of the New Covenant principle.

The next two chapters, in which we shall be taking a closer look at the New Covenant, are instructive in this regard.

Chapter Four
The New Covenant: a human phenomenon?

The first explicit[1] reference to the New Covenant in the Bible appears in Jeremiah 31:31-34. As the Wycliffe Bible Commentary suggests (page 679), the concept of the New Covenant is Jeremiah's most important contribution to biblical thought. This passage reads,

> Behold the days come, saith the Lord, that I will make a new covenant with the house of Israel, and with the house of Judah: Not according to the covenant that I made with their fathers in the day that I took them by the hand to bring them out of the land of Egypt; which my covenant they brake, although I was an husband unto them, saith the Lord: But this shall be the covenant that I will make with the house of Israel; After those days, saith the Lord, I will put my law in their inward parts, and write it in their hearts; and will be their God, and they shall be my people.
> And they shall teach no more every man his neighbour, and every man his brother, saying, Know the Lord: for they shall all know me, from the least of them, unto the greatest of them, saith the Lord: for I will forgive their iniquity, and I will remember their sin no more.

In this prophecy the author declares the intention of God to abandon his original "contract" with the nation of Israel which had proven defective, in favour of a new, more personalized, that is, individualistic agreement.

Clearly, the characteristic quality of this proposed covenant is its innateness, its individualism. Against the old covenant's preoccupation with Israel as a nation, the new covenant emphasizes God's concern for the individual Jew (also consider Ezekiel 18).

The intensely personal, spontaneous and indeed, spiritual nature of this covenant, is obvious in the fact that it is designated to the realm of the heart, our innermost being.

Likewise, it is obvious that in contrast to the Sinai covenant, the New Covenant is not to be presented in written form. It is a spiritual discourse, not a literal document. It is invisible, not open to public viewing and scrutiny. It consists in interaction between God and the individual. It is private. The theme and focus of the New Covenant is individual faith and responsibility.

This individualism - God's overriding concern with and interest in the secrets of people's hearts - is evident in other parts of the Old Testament (1Sam 16:7; Ps 44:20,21; Isa 19:13) but it comes to the fore, albeit inconsistently, in Jesus' teaching, as recorded in the Bible - the teaching to which the so-called "New Testament" writings attest.

In the gospels Jesus is presented as the inaugurator and ratifier of the New Covenant (Matthew 26:28; Mark 14:24; Luke 22:20;). Accordingly, his teachings demonstrate the conviction that God is primarily concerned with matters of the heart (Matthew 15:1-20; Mark 7:1-23).

This motif, particularly evident in the gospel attributed to John, is at the heart of Christian spirituality: as John 4:24 puts it,

> God is Spirit: and they that worship him must worship him in spirit and in truth.

(note that I have followed the Wycliffe commentary and dropped "a", hence " God is Spirit", not "a Spirit").

The individualistic phenomenon identified as the New Covenant in the Bible, is therefore key to the Christian ethic.

The point I wish to make here is that this phenomenon is not unique to Christianity.

There is substantial evidence which suggests that virtually the same phenomenon - expressed differently and identified by other terms and titles - operates in other religions, some of them much older than Christianity.

Indeed, it shall be seen that this individualistic dynamic which Jeremiah referred to as the New Covenant, can be seen as the essential positive element in a perennial pattern of degeneration and renewal which characterizes the history of all religions.

101

In a discussion entitled "Origins of Religion", Peter Brow[2], attests to this pattern of degeneration and renewal as he argues

> ...the case for an original monotheism and worship
> through animal sacrifice, with subsequent degeneration
> into polytheism...

Brow notes that this biblical hypothesis is much easier to fit into "the recurring cycles of history" than the "gradual upward evolution of religion" proposed by secular Darwinian anthropologists.

It does indeed appear that history itself bears witness to the universality, rather than uniqueness, of the phenomenon of individually-oriented religion. It shall be seen that historically this dynamic has operated as a counterbalance to the inevitable deterioration which plagues all religious movements. The degeneration that The World's Religions (the text quoted above, subsequently TWR) calls priestcraft.

You will recall that I introduced the term priestcraft in chapter 3 sect. ii. There I dealt with the emergence and establishment of the *ekklesia* (the Church) in Christianity, and how this coincided with Jesus' followers losing sight of the true focus of his teaching, that is, the inevitability and integrity of individual faith and the consequent need for tolerance[3].

Priestcraft you see, undermines individual faith. It is group oriented. Essentially, this term signifies the rise of a group of people who claim to control access to God[4].

My account here of the emergence of the *ekklesia* and the unfolding of the other historical factors which I believe are the true basis of the fundamentalist terror of the Bible, is therefore largely a recounting of the operation of priestcraft within the Christian faith.

It is also a recounting of the operation of the regenerating New Covenant - to the extent that the operation of this phenomenon in the history of Christianity has also been highlighted here. Remember, both elements make up the cycles of religious history.

Let us now consider a case-history which demonstrates this pattern of degeneration and renewal prior to the Christian era. Brow supplies the following account of the degeneration of the Brahmin priesthood of India[5].

The clearest documented account of this degeneration appears in the history of the

Brahmin priesthood of India. The earliest group of Vedic hymns called the Rig Veda were first collected in an oral form, say about 1500 BC, as the Aryan tribes were invading northwestern India. The collection may have been the work of the first regular priests. At this time sacrifice could still be offered by any Aryan, and priesthood was by inclination, probably on a part-time basis. Under settled conditions the power of the priests tended to increase. They suggested that unless the right sacrifices were offered the gods would be displeased, and therefore only highly trained priests could learn the prayers and rituals which were necessary.

Some specialization began, and a school of singing priests (Udgatri) arose who chanted the special hymns for each sacrificial occasion. Their collection of 1,225 hymns (the Sama Veda) were all from the Rig Veda, except for the seventy-five new ones. Then a third book called the Yajur Veda was produced by a class of priests who did the actual offering of sacrifice. Their collection was mainly the ritual formulae muttered in a low voice during the various stages of the sacrifice. Thus by about 900 BC there were at least three groups of priests with their own special duties and training schools. The priests had leisure to study and teach, and knowledge brought power. It was only natural that the priestly schools should produce notes and commentaries on their books (the same kind of thing happens today). The material is called Brahmanas, which includes explanation of the hymns, the rituals of sacrifice and the duties of the priests. The study of this material produced an elaborate scholasticism.

By the time of the Brahmanas (about 800-700 BC), the Brahmins had become a hereditary priesthood in charge of all sacrificial duties, for which they were paid fees by the people. The Brahmins were now suggesting

that by the right sacrifices, which they alone could offer,
they could procure the favour of the gods, various
temporal blessings, and a good place in heaven. Gods,
men, governments, all were under priestly control.

Brow goes on to mention the Atharva Veda, the fourth Veda to be
compiled. He notes that because of its lateness and the low ethical
quality of its contents, this Veda is still not recognized in some parts
of south India. Most of the stanzas of the Atharva Veda consist of
charms and incantations for magical purposes, and shows how easily
priestcraft degenerates into witchcraft. Note the use of the Psalms and
Apocryphal books in a similar fashion by many Christians, most
recently the proponents of the Bible Code, which is based on Jewish
mystical Kabalah tradition.

The similarity between these developments in the Brahmin
priesthood and what has taken place in Christianity is immediately
obvious[6].

Note that Brow's summary of the extent of the Brahmin's power
by the time of the Brahmanas, can be transferred without any
modification whatsoever, to the context of Christian history, and is
particularly applicable to the medieval church:

Gods, men, governments, all were under priestly
control.

Now what does the Brahmin case-history have to say about the
regenerative stage of the cycles of religious history, to which the New
Covenant phenomenon is key?

Much indeed, for the Brahmin story also bears witness to the
perennial renewal that counters priestcraft.

Hence we are told that the excesses of the Brahmins were checked
by the sixth century religious revolution, which saw "a tidal wave of
revolt" rise against the priestcraft of that era.

In fact, Brow refers to this revolution as a "great movement of
freedom for the human mind", and compares its importance for world
history with that of the Renaissance and Reformation in Europe 2,000
years later.

He might just as appropriately have compared it with that era which saw the birth of Christianity though.

You see, in his emphasis on personal faith, Luther was not only preceded by Jesus of Nazareth: he had a predecessor of at least 2,000 years (2900 seems preferable; see below) in Zoroaster - more correctly Zarathushtra, the prophet of ancient Persia.

Many scholars (including Brow) date Zoroaster around 600 BC, but linguistic and sociological data is persuading more of them to accept a date around 1500 BC[7]. This would put him among the earliest of the great prophets of the world's religions.

This would also mean one of two things: either that Brow's dating of the wave of religious revolt with which he associates Zoroaster is wrong (too late), or else that the dating of the revolution is correct, but Zoroaster himself was not directly involved in it, that is, the revolution was prompted by a revival of his teaching.

The latter scenario is more probable. ISBE notes[8] that the Magi "adopted" Zoroaster's teaching, and suggests that this accounts for the late dating of the prophet.

Accordingly, the reader is advised to reject Brow's suggestion that the preaching of the eighth-century prophets of Israel (about 740 BC onward, with the refrain from Jeremiah and Ezekiel a century or so later) is one obvious possible cause of the "Zoroastrian reformation". This suggestion is based on the later, less probable dating of Zoroaster around 600 BC. It is in fact more likely that the eighth century prophets of Israel were influenced by Zarathushtra (perhaps via the Magi), not the other way around.

The main point though, is that Zoroaster's views were basically identical with those that constitute the New Covenant phenomenon; they are summarized as follows:

> All men (and women, both sexes have the same duties in Zoroastrianism) have a personal responsibility to choose between Good and evil. On the basis of the exercise of their free-will, men will be judged in the hereafter." Those whose good thoughts, words and deeds outweigh the evil will go to heaven, regardless of their social status; those whose evil thoughts words and deeds outweigh the good will go to hell, again regardless of their social status. This moral democracy offended the

established priests and princes who had considered
paradise their sole preserve.

The characteristic feature of this teaching, as TWR rightly
observes, is its emphasis on personal religion - the theme of the New
Covenant.

My chief concern here is not to say whether the earliest recorded
individually-oriented religious revival took place among the Persians
or the Jews. My purpose is to establish that this kind of revival is as
old as religion itself, and has been occurring repeatedly throughout the
length and breadth of human history. It is not a Jewish or Persian
phenomenon; it is a human phenomenon. It is as natural and
inevitable as the degeneration it counters.

Jeremiah spoke of this phenomenon in the language and context of
the Jewish culture and faith (the language of the covenant), but this
religious dynamic is older than Judaism. Apparently, it is as old as
humanity.

It is important that we have this historical perspective on the New
Covenant, for then we are better able to put the Christian
understanding of it, that is, the "New Testament" writers' witness to it,
into proper perspective.

From the outset, an important assertion of Christians has been that
Christianity is unique. This claim is reflected in and based on such
"New Testament" passages as Acts 4:12 which, referring to Jesus
declares,

> Neither is there salvation in any other: for there is
> none other name under heaven given among men,
> whereby we must be saved.

This exclusionist posture - an essential element in the intimidating
perception of the Bible being discouraged here - is at the heart of the
evangelical motif. Arguably, the vast majority of Christians, certainly
fundamentalist Christians, believe it is their duty to evangelize the
world (to convert people everywhere to Christianity) because they
alone have the truth.

I certainly believed that, and I quoted Acts 4:12 rather vociferously
while campaigning for Jesus in open-air meetings.

Well, the recurrence and centrality of the New Covenant principle throughout humanity's religious history - the virtual universality of this principle with which Jesus of Nazareth is so crucially linked - undermines that proposition.

The New Covenant is not unique. Indeed, it would appear that it is only Christians' ignorance of what the New Covenant actually is, that sustains them in their illusion about its uniqueness, and the uniqueness of Christianity as a whole.

The objection may be made though, that the claim of the uniqueness of Christianity is not based on the role of the New Covenant in Christianity, but rather on the uniqueness of the person of Christ. Christopher Lamb's suggestion[9] that

> The Christian claim is that Christ is unique:
> Christianity is not.

is a semantic evasion of this kind.

This and similar objections could only be voiced by persons who, among other things, do not appreciate the centrality of the New Covenant phenomenon to any sound interpretation of the life and mission of Jesus Christ. The fact is, the two cannot be divorced. If for no other reason, such an objection is therefore pointless.

However, arguments for the universality of the ethic that Jesus espoused are not only founded on the biblical association of Jesus with the New Covenant. There are at least two other biblical concepts which are closely akin to, or better, almost identical with that of the New Covenant, but which also did not originate within Christianity and so betray the "commonness" of Jesus' teachings, and by extension, the "commonness" of the Bible's inspiration. These are the concept of the Logos and the concept of conscience.

The Greek term Logos, translated "Word" appears in John 1:1 where it refers to Jesus himself. Many Christians, particularly fundamentalists, also believe that this is a reference to the Bible, and therefore refer to the Bible as "the word that became flesh". I distinctly recall seeing that being done by a preaching minister on at least one occasion.

However, the author of John's gospel probably had more in mind than the Bible or any other body of scriptures when he wrote this passage.

What many Christians do not know, is that the origin of the Logos concept dates back to the Greek philosopher Heraclitus, who lived some 500 years before Jesus of Nazareth[10].

Heraclitus viewed the universe as fashioned by a fiery element, the all penetrating reason (Logos) of which the souls, spirits or minds (essentially, the inner-man) of men are a part.

So although logos was used by the Greeks of biblical times to refer to the spoken word, and even the written word sometimes, the manner in which it is used here (as a reference to God, and his creative activity, v.3) suggests that the author's focus was not simply on audible or visual words, but rather that he was employing this term as Heraclitus had done, in reference to reason or *thought* - the spiritual or creative origin of words.

Words convey thought, but they are not thought, meaning or purpose in themselves: they do not constitute the creative, purposeful and rational nucleus of reality that can be called God.

The translation of Logos as "Word" in John 1:1 is therefore rather misleading since the author is probably referring to the concept of reason or thought.

A further indication of this is the relatively well known fact that Heraclitus' teachings were incorporated into Jewish theology, primarily through the philosopher/theologian Philo Judaeus who, not surprisingly, was a contemporary of Jesus and his disciples[11].

Philo's influence on Christianity is scarcely disputed today among informed Christians, and John 1:1 is probably the verse most frequently cited as an example of his, and by extension Heraclitus' contribution to Christian doctrine.

The epistle to the Hebrews is another primary example. This entire epistle reflects Philonic influence - some might even say derivation. ISBE notes that the style, terminology and pattern of thought are clearly Philo's.

Of particular relevance to our subject though, is Hebrews 4:12. Here the unity of the Logos concept and that of the New Covenant is obvious. This passage reads,

> For the word of God is quick, and powerful, and
> sharper than any two-edged sword, piercing even to the

dividing asunder of soul and spirit, and of the joints and
marrow, and is a discerner of the thoughts and intents of
the heart.

This verse recalls the words of Romans 2:12-16, where the same
principle of spirit-oriented judgment is set out. In verse 15 reference
is made to the concept of conscience, the other virtual synonym of the
New Covenant that I shall be looking at here.

We shall be turning to that discussion of the concept of conscience
shortly, but first I want to share an item of evidence which
demonstrates that emphasis on the universality of Jesus' teachings as
borne out by the Logos concept in scripture, is nothing new to
Christianity.

I draw your attention to the words of Justin Martyr[12], the most
notable Christian apologist of the second century. He once wrote,

Christ is the Logos in whom every race of men
shared. Those who lived in accordance with Logos, true
reason, are Christians, even though they were regarded,
as atheists; for example, Socrates and Heraclitus among
the Greeks.

Clearly, this prominent Christian's perception of Jesus' person and
mission was more universalistic and embracing than that advocated by
fundamentalists.

Now for the concept of conscience.

The English word "conscience" also has its origins in classical
Greek usage. It translates the Greek noun *syneidesis*.

Some scholars have concluded that *syneidesis* was invented by the
Stoics, because of a few references to this term in the writings of
certain Stoic philosophers.

However, stronger evidence indicates that the noun *syneidesis*
simply evolved in every day usage from forms of the verb *synoida*;
these appear frequently in a variety of Greek writings, popular as well
as technical, dating back to the 6th century B.C.

Evidently, in typical linguistic fashion, by the 1st century B.C., the
verb describing an action had developed into a noun form designating
the agent in the human makeup that performs the action[13].

109

The literal meaning of the verb *synoida* is "know in common with". It may simply denote "being conscious" or "being aware" of something. It is significant that the verb appears in both reflexive and non-reflexive form. In its non-reflexive form *synoida* appears as *synoida tini ti* or *synoida tinos ti* or *synoida peri tinos* and literally means "have knowledge of something with another (as an eyewitness)." Its general use is to indicate knowing about another person, as a witness for or against him.

It is the reflexive form of the verb, *synoida emauto*, literally "I know with myself", that we are most concerned with though, for this moves closer to the meaning of the noun. Here the one who knows and the one who shares the knowledge or witnesses to it are the same person.

Something very important happened around the 1st century B.C. - interestingly, at about the time of Jesus' advent - when the verb form *synoida* shifted to the noun form *syneidesis*.

Literally, *syneidesis* is "the self that knows with itself." It is significant though, that *syneidesis* is not merely another action performed by the self; it is now an agent within the self. The development of the noun form signaled the recognition of an alter ego, another self within the self that observes the self and then testifies as to what it sees.

It should be noted that while the tendency is to see the sole function of conscience as the making of moral judgments, the term *syneidesis* actually has a broader meaning than that of a moral witness.

As stated above, *syneidesis* literally means the self knowing with or observing itself; the basic factor here is self-awareness, not morality. While self-awareness usually has moral dimensions, this is not necessarily or invariably the case.

Self-awareness covers more than awareness of one's moral status. Literally, *syneidesis* can include all that belongs to the self engaged in the act of reflecting upon itself.

The close relation of this Greek concept to the Jewish New Covenant phenomenon is borne out in passages such as Romans 2:12-16, mentioned above. As ISBE[14] puts it,

What Paul appears to have done is to recognize the

inner agent known to the Greeks as conscience, but to
give his own version of the content of its testimony.

His version of its content would obviously be his understanding of
the invisible etchings of the New Covenant, probably coloured in
some measure by traditional Judaism's ethos.

What is significant is that the apostle did not modify the universal
character of conscience, but like the Greeks, advances the view that
this phenomenon is in all human beings, even the Gentiles who "have
not the law".

There is a passage sometimes attributed to the Stoic philosopher
Epictetus[15] which speaks of conscience and is strikingly paralleled in
Paul's reference in Galations 3:24-26 to the New Covenant era of
faith, initiated by and prevailing in Christ.

The passage attributed to Epictetus reads,

> When we were children our parents handed us over to
> a nursery slave who should watch over us everywhere
> lest harm befall us. But when we were grown up, God
> hands us over to the conscience implanted in us, to
> protect us. Let us not in any way despise it's protection
> for should we do so we shall be both ill-pleasing to God
> and have our own conscience as an enemy.

Its parallel in Paul's epistle to the Galations reads,

> Wherefore the law was our schoolmaster to bring us
> unto Christ, that we might be justified by faith. But after
> that faith is come, we are no longer under a schoolmaster.
> For ye are all children of God by faith in Jesus Christ.

There can be no doubt that the authoritative (guiding) reality
identified by Paul as "Christ", "faith" and "faith in Christ" alternately,
is the same phenomenon which the other author identifies as
conscience.

And so the evidence accumulates against the uniqueness of the
New Covenant phenomenon, against the uniqueness of the teachings
of the Bible, and ultimately, against the uniqueness of Christianity on

the whole.

In the biblical writers' usage, that is in the terms by which they refer to the nature and workings of the "inner man" (and within the context of their concept of salvation, that is, the "regenerated" psyche) the New Covenant phenomenon is also associated, and or identified with the concept of "the Comforter" (Greek *paraclete*) and "the Anointing" (Greek *chrisma*)[16], and I would not be surprised to find that these latter concepts also originated outside of Judaism and Christianity or are at least paralleled elsewhere.

Pursuing these concepts here would only be academic though. I am satisfied that sufficient evidence has already been presented to support the universality of the New Covenant and the implicit non-threatening, embracing "commonness" of the Bible - its origin and form (inspired scripture) and its content (authoritative teaching).

It will be more advantageous for us to look more closely at the concept of conscience and the benefits that stand to be derived from the fullest possible understanding of this phenomenon.

You see, ultimately, what I am proposing here is that the New Covenant of Judaism and Christianity is a metaphor (one of many such religious metaphors - the Greeks' *Logos* and perhaps, the ancient Egyptians' *Ma'at*[17], called *Hokmot* by the Hebrews, are others) for that phenomenon which in modern times is widely known as conscience.

I am suggesting that conscience, which seems to be viewed predominantly as a secular concept today (and one advantage of this is that it is not as easy for any particular interest group to claim a monopoly on this phenomenon) is the medium by which the personal reality we call God communicates with all humanity.

In expressly religious terms, I am proposing that conscience be seen as the primary medium of humanity's "salvation".

For me, overcoming the terror and appreciating the beauty of the Bible or any other externally-oriented authoritative medium of truth means learning to understand and trust ourselves - our consciences.

Chapter Five
Conscience Vindicated

The views on the phenomenon of conscience that I present in this chapter consist mainly of inferences drawn from my own study of religion - especially Christianity - and my assessment of human behaviour in general.

While I am not (yet) a credentialed authority on behavioural science or the psyche of man, I have given considerable thought to these matters and have benefited significantly in my studies from the treatment of these subjects by more learned persons. I am particularly indebted to the ISBE article on conscience cited in the previous chapter.

Special mention must again be made of the text Language and Communication1 and other materials that are a part of my current studies in Linguistics at the University of the West Indies. This field of study has much to offer persons studying "book-centred" faiths such as Christianity. The point I wish to make here is that there is some academic and objective basis to the views on conscience which I am presenting.

Still, in keeping with the individualistic focus of this work, I must remind the reader that the validity, utility and justification of my understanding of the nature and workings of conscience does not rest solely on its objectivity.

The views expressed here are not only valid as academic positions but also - and in a personal sense, that is, for me, more so - as my own conscience-oriented corroboration of what can be called the testimony of "common sense"; my views have validity as my *own*, individual, assent to the universal testimony of conscience.

In commending my views on conscience to the reader's consideration therefore, my appeal is to both empirical (objective) and intuitive (subjective) evidence, and my hope is to encourage this balanced approach by others.

According to ISBE, conscience is the self engaged in the act of observing itself. The point was made that the essential component in

113

syneidesis (the Greek term behind conscience) is self-awareness, not morality.

The neutrality of this view coincides automatically with that of one of the main theories on conscience which modern ethics has developed, significantly, "...without appealing to supernatural principles" (note that here we have some degree of consensus among secular and religious authorities, arrived at apparently from antithetical positions).

According to Colliers Encyclopedia[2], two main theories on conscience prevail in modern ethics. There is intuitionism, which agrees with the theological doctrine that there exists a direct and imperative certainty of right and wrong, but describes this so-called "moral sense" as a plain fact of moral nature; and there is empiricism which, basing its premises on the evidence of experience, rejects the theological idea that there is any immediate conviction of right and wrong and suggests that conscience is simply the cumulative inference from past experience directing human future conduct.

According to this view, the authority of conscience is not universal or absolute, but varies with circumstances and is ever subject to revision.

ISBE's literary-historical interpretation of conscience (based on the Greek *syneidesis*) is clearly compatible with the empirical theory. It can be inferred from both of these concepts that initially, - when we are born - conscience is neutral on moral issues. This neutrality of embryonic conscience suggests that conscience is primarily concerned with the mediation or processing of information ([con]science), or knowledge for the benefit of the individual.

The ethical dimension to or implications of this knowledge then appears as a secondary development, which occurs as elementary knowledge is coloured by experience. Since our experiences all differ to some degree, the evaluations or values that result are therefore relative, not fixed.

It is this relativity of conscience and hence of morality, evident in both religious and secular studies, that many people, and especially fundamentalists, find unnerving. It allows for too much ambiguity, too much uncertainty.

It is the difficulty involved in coming to terms with this ambiguity and a resulting denial or else ignoring of the relativity of ethics that has led Christians to turn to the seemingly more certain and or inflexible canon or standard of morality that is scripture - things written. This in turn has brought about what is perhaps the greatest and most tragic irony of fundamentalist Christianity - its marginalization of the concept and role of conscience.

In practice, fundamentalism with its idealistic emphasis on the Bible, tends to relegate conscience to the status of an irresolute, ambiguous moral guide - a vague inner light that at its best is overly-scrupulous, and at its worst abandons humanity to all manner of licentiousness and vice.

Of course, there is some truth in this view: the witness of conscience is often ambiguous; but the irresoluteness or ambiguity of conscience is not as thorough, as unrelenting nor as hazardous to humanity's acquaintance with and understanding of truth and righteousness as fundamentalists suggest.

The ambiguity and irresoluteness of conscience only appears that hazardous when it is set against the idyllic, artificial and inflexible perception of truth and righteousness that obtains in fundamentalism and is epitomized in its perception of the Bible as an inerrant and infallible guide.

The fact is that the ambiguity of conscience is merely a reflection of the actual inescapable ambiguity that evolves as elemental knowledge - what we hear, see, feel and so on, is coloured by the myriad, temporal and transient hues of individual experience.

The ambiguity is therefore inevitable; it is as inevitable as our individualistic diversity - the fact that we experience reality first and foremost as individuals.

Conscience, that by which we "know", that is, identify and understand, ourselves and the reality (environment, circumstances, society) of which we are a part is primarily an individualistic phenomenon.

Now, there are those who stress the social dimension of conscience (as perhaps, in the Caribbean Conference of Churches conscientization project[2]) and there is merit in this.

Conscience does have a collective, universal dimension as well as a unique individualistic one, and I could even accept the suggestion of advocates of "cosmic consciousness" that there is a level of consciousness at which the two dimensions of conscience are unified;

a level at which the individual's perception is or becomes fused with the perceptions of all humanity (also consider Carl Jung's theory of the "collective unconscious").

For the most part though, we experience reality - or in any case are essentially most conscious of what we experience - at the individual level. And my reality, my truth (coloured among other things, by my parentage and my wider educational and socio-cultural background) will naturally differ from yours in some way.

Even identical twins whose experiences are mostly shared, or at least shared in the earliest and most enduringly impressionable years of their lives - from birth to about six years old - develop views of reality that differ to some extent. The differences may be great or small.

I am acutely aware of this myself because I have an identical twin brother , Wayne, whose view of reality is not identical with my own.

It is this inevitable, natural divergence of experiences, opinions and views that accounts for the ambiguity that confronts mankind (both at the individual and the social level) as we grapple with moral questions.

Fundamentalistic insistence on "black and white" clarity in ethical matters does not change this. It cannot and will not make the ambiguity go away.

Rather, such indifference and insensitivity to the ambiguity of moral questions which conscience reflects, leads to an oversimplification of the issues, stereotyping and rash judgments.

Ultimately, and this is the irony, it leads to an erosion or impairment of conscience, and the immersion of individuals in the very ambiguity and confusion they seek to avoid.

Again I refer readers' attention to the Jim Jones, David Koresh and similar tragedies. The moral insensitivity, callousness, confusion and perversity which persons perpetrating these tragedies demonstrated was the end result of their failure to cope with the ambiguity of ethical issues. It was the result of their imposition of simplistic solutions on the complex construct that is morality.

This is how fundamentalism in its insistence on the "plain meaning" and the "inerrancy and infallibility" of the Bible, turns on those who embrace it.

Fundamentalist detractors would say, "Oh, but persons like Jones

116

and Koresh are wicked and deluded. They interpret the Bible to suit themselves; they are following their own agenda. You can't blame the Bible for that!"

However I am not blaming the Bible. My argument is directed against a particular idealistic, historically unsound perception of the Bible that leads persons interpreting the Bible into thinking that their interpretations are unquestionable, above ambiguity, perfect, or as they might say, inerrant and infallible!

As I pointed out before, I agree with 2Timothy 3:16 which says that scripture is profitable. I am not denying that. I am urging a balanced approach to and understanding of the Bible's profitability.

You see, the truth is that whether it is done consciously or unconsciously, we all interpret the Bible subjectively to some degree. There is some element of individuality in all our interpretations of scripture. Our consciences - the interpreters and relaters of our individual experiences - make this inevitable.

This is natural. God in his infinite wisdom has made us this way. There is nothing wrong with this.

The problem comes when the individual starts thinking that his or her interpretation of the Bible, or his or her understanding of reality in general, is the *only* correct or accurate one.

The doctrine of the inerrancy and infallibility of the Bible leads implicitly to this exclusionist conclusion: if the Bible is inerrant and infallible it follows that once the individual (or group) interprets it accurately, his or her (or their) interpretation is inerrant and infallible, and by extension, all differing interpretations are incorrect.

Acknowledgment and mindfulness of the individualism of conscience - its orientation in individual experience - and hence its relativity and limitations, checks this exclusionism for it highlights our subjectivity and the consequent futility of seeking a single correct interpretation of the Bible.

This futility is especially obvious when we see the divinely inspired Bible as being a product of conscience itself - when we consider that divine revelation comes to us via human, temporal, limited, subjective vessels.

As the writer of that exceptional treatise on love that is 1Corinthians 13 observes,

For we know in part, and we prophesy in part...For now we see through a glass darkly; but then face to face: now I know in part; but then shall I know even as also I am known.

The greatest need of humanity therefore, is to be mindful of the limits of our knowledge. It is to be mindful of the limits that attach to and are brought to the fore by conscience. We need to be mindful of conscience's nature and function as an individualistic phenomenon and the implications of this individualism for social interaction - the ambiguity that ensues.

I believe that this mindfulness is essentially what modern critical analysis calls enlightened intelligence. This concept of conscience is featured in the Colliers' article mentioned above as a compromise of sorts which modern ethics has reached between its recognition of the varieties of moral experience (empiricism) and the moral demand for imperative validity of universal principles (intuitionism).

Enlightened intelligence is an altruistic approach whereby modern ethics emphasizes the primacy of the social welfare and conscience is described as "social-mindedness controlling willful individualism".

This altruism includes but is also transcended by perfectionist ethics' identification of conscience as "morally integrated consciousness, the expression of the most mature and harmonious insight". According to this view,

The authority of this most enlightened intelligence in conduct combines resolution with tolerance and self criticism.

The paradox is obvious; mindfulness of our social obligations is rooted in mindfulness of our obligation toward ourselves. Tolerance of what we perceive as others' limited understanding is essentially tied to acknowledgment and acceptance (tolerance) of the limits of our own understanding.

The question is asked, "How can we love others as ourselves, if we do not love ourselves?"

The question, framed to bring conscience into focus is: how can we claim to love ourselves and yet do not accept the limits of our knowledge and experiences?

This is the paradox (not a contradiction) that characterizes conscience; a paradox which revolves around the coexistent universal and unique dimensions of conscience mentioned above.

And let us not confuse the individualistic uniqueness of conscience with the *ekklesiatically* inspired and oriented claims of uniqueness of fundamentalist Christianity and other fundamentalist religious and or philosophical systems. The latter uniqueness is associated with priestcraft.

To put this in terms that should be more familiar to Christians, it is the very individuality, the limitedness or if you will, fallibility of conscience that warrants grace (a much used but misunderstood term among fundamentalists) in the social context, that is, in our dealings with others.

Grace by this understanding is simply synonymous with tolerance.

Accordingly, the gracious or Godly individual is the one who recognizes that moral ambiguity - those grey areas that surround questions of righteousness and sin in Church affairs or right and wrong in everyday living - are not manufactured by liberal theologians, willful Christians or atheists.

This ambiguity is a natural consequence of the diverse outlooks of our consciences. We must learn to live with this. We must learn to compromise with each other; to graciously agree to disagree.

In chapter 3 section iii I pointed out that it is not our differences which divide us but rather the attitude toward or manner in which we view those differences and seek to resolve them. Accordingly then, the essence of Christianity would be a conciliatory attitude to our differences.

As conscience itself causes us to recognize the inevitability of differences, and our own limitations in understanding those differences at the individual level, the limitations of our individual knowledge - each person's peculiar measure of faith, so to speak (Rom. 12:3) - we are inclined and obligated to exercise restraint in judging ourselves and to be tolerant of others.

Several passages in the Bible address this matter of the limitations of conscience. Among these are the entire chapter of 1Corinthians 8 and chapter 10:23-33.

In these passages Paul suggests that in relation to meats offered to idols, the conscience of some is weak, that is, overly scrupulous (according to ISBE the weak conscience's testimony may be "uncertain, confused, or in error..").

Paul's response gives us a further insight into the workings of conscience. It is clear that personally, he does not agree with the witness of the weak conscience, but still he cautions those with strong consciences not to tempt their weaker brethren, or induce the violation of the weak conscience.

In the words of ISBE, Paul suggests that

> ...those whose consciences are strong need to respect the consciences of the weak. One whose conscience is strong need not be bound by the weak. There is a liberty of conscience that is not overruled by another man's scruples.

Of course, there is the possibility that the weak conscience may be strengthened through education. It was perhaps toward this end that the point was made that "an idol is nothing" and "there is none other God but one".

The same concern for the scruples of the weak are expressed in Rom. 14; here though the word conscience (*syneidesis*) is replaced by the word faith (*pistis*), demonstrating the close relation between faith and conscience in the Bible. Also consider the intimate relation between faith and conscience expressed in 1Tim. 1:18,19 and 3:9.

What we are dealing with here is our perceptions of right and wrong; those concepts which the Bible calls "righteousness" and "sin", among other things.

I shall not go into these in any great detail here: I believe it is sufficient to say that a truly biblical concept of sin - one which relies on the original Hebrew and Greek words behind this term - would not be as simplistic, fixed or precise as the traditional blanket usage of the English term "sin" suggests.

Professor Bromiley, the General Editor of ISBE opens his article on Sin[4] by declaring that,

> The complexity of sin is illustrated by the great number of Hebrew words for it.

There is need for a more thorough understanding of this term "sin" in evangelical circles. Traditional simplistic concepts such as that common among those ambitiously labeled "Full-Gospel" ministers tend to be deficient.

So there is some difficulty involved in the elevation of fallible conscience to a place of final authority in Christianity. However that risk is not created by conscience: conscience merely brings it to the fore.

The difficulty or ambiguity is the natural consequence of the individualistic diversity in which God in his infinite wisdom has made humankind.

It is an unavoidable difficulty. Insisting that the Bible is inerrant and infallible - and as a natural consequence, implying that there exists an inerrant and infallible will of God that people may (or must) obey - is merely a form of denial, and as such, compounds the difficulty.

Persons who do this (especially church leaders, who must bear the bulk of the responsibility) are being insensitive to the exigencies of the present - the rigor of real life and the rigidness of words that do not allow for precise definition of our every act and thought.

Their literalistic standards allow little or no margin for error. Yet we know that at the level of individual conscience, the level of immediate experience, the will of God is more easily accessed in principle than it is in particulars.

There really are no easy answers to the deepest questions of life, no infallible blue prints on morality or fail-proof formulae for righteous and successful living.

My former belief that there was such a "will of God" led me to the place where I was endeavoring to be doing exactly what God expected of me in my every waking moment. Fundamentalism predisposes one to this unenlightened desire by its suggestion that this perfect will of God is accessible to mankind through God's perfect Word: the inerrant and infallible Bible.

This is why I started to write the book entitled "What on earth are you doing?" My intention was to challenge Christians to make their every waking moment count for the Glory of God. I had an acute desire to be living that way myself. I had an extreme desire to redeem whatever time I have on this earth. I am still a bit of a workaholic but now I feel less anxious about "playing hard" too.

Many fundamentalists go through this "will of God anxiety". Consider the number of books that have been written on "finding the will of God" in recent decades: you might notice a proliferation.

I saw others going through the same thing years ago, and I see people (some very near and dear to me) going through it now. "I just want to do the will of God" they would say, believing that this will is clearly expressed in the Bible and that they need only find it.

I know first-hand the earnestness and actual torment these people sometimes go through in their efforts to discover and conform to this perfect will. I know the sense of guilt that they often feel when they sense that they have fallen short of this perfect will; the sense of condemnation and fear that accompanies any violation of the inerrant and infallible word of God.

I am simultaneously moved by these persons' sincerity, pained by their naiveté, and outraged over their exploitation at the hands of persons who know better.

Church leaders do better to openly acknowledge the priority of conscience in the determination of Christian doctrine and practice, for even when some claim that the allegedly "inerrant and infallible" Bible is their final authority, it is clear that they are ultimately dependent on their consciences (those who still seem to have one) for the interpretation that is given to the Bible.

This is why there are so many different understandings of the much mooted "plain meaning" of the Bible. The Bible is capable of a variety of interpretations, first and foremost because it is itself a by-product of conscience - as noted earlier.

This conclusion that the Bible is a by-product of conscience does not preclude recognition of a divine origin of the Bible. What it requires is a greater acknowledgment of the human element in the Bible, or else for us to see conscience as having its roots in divinity.

At any rate, it means conceding that the reference to the Spirit of God which "itself beareth witness with our spirit" is in the final analysis, a reference to the operation of conscience. Conscience will then be viewed as a divine-human dialogue.

This idea will be repulsive to fundamentalists precisely because it proposes an essential kinship - even unity - between God and man.

Given my former orientation in fundamentalist theocentric (God-centred) thinking, it took me a while to get comfortable with any kind of anthropocentric (man-centred or humanist) religious ideas myself.

Fundamentalists are warned against embracing any kind of theology (or anthropology) which puts mankind at the centre of the universe or in any way represents human beings as being divine - even potentially so. This aspiration, it is argued, was the original sin of Adam and Eve; their desire to be like God.

Alternately fundamentalist authorities charge that it is the tendency of degenerate humanity to fashion a perfect God after our own imperfect image.

Related arguments are used in defense of the doctrine of the inerrancy and infallibility of the Bible. For example, it is suggested that any challenge to this doctrine is an attempt to bring God down to man's level.

The relation of these arguments is no great mystery. The plain fact of the matter is that the idealistic and intimidating concept of the Bible that I am challenging here stems from an idealistic and intimidating concept of God. A concept of God that totally extricates him from the realm of human experience; a theology which in fact makes God the antithesis of everything considered human.

According to this theology conscience is basically a "fleshy" human faculty, part of the degenerate, errant and fallible nature of man and hence distinct from the inerrant and infallible Spirit of God - to whom only the redeemed have access.

The redeemed are of course those who believe in the inerrancy and infallibility of the Bible and conform to its teachings - as prescribed by the traditions or interpretations of the relevant ecclesiastical authority.

Yet, as I study the concept of conscience in the Bible, and similar concepts like that of the Logos (Greek), Millot (Phoenecian)[5] and Ma'at (Egyptian), I find it difficult to avoid the conclusion that there is considerable biblical and extra-biblical support for anthropocentric ideas about the divine - or theocentric views about humanity. This matter will be discussed further in the closing chapter.

For now, just let me remind readers that the elevation, or better, *acknowledgment* of conscience that I am proposing here does not undermine the claims made for scripture in 2Timothy 3:16, namely that it is inspired and profitable. To suggest that elevating conscience means undermining the Bible's profitability is to create a false dilemma.

Recognition of the priority of conscience over or alongside the Bible and respect, indeed reverence for the Bible, are not mutually exclusive positions. It is clear to me that the Bible has tremendous ethical and historical utility, validity and authority.

However, its authority is not final. The Bible does not interpret itself. The Bible is subject to interpretation at the level of conscience.

Insistence on the final authority of the Bible is mostly a device by which fundamentalist churchmen cloak their own preferences and prejudices and disclaim or sidestep their responsibility for the interpretations they choose to extract from the Bible.

I am urging a more transparent and balanced approach to biblical interpretation. This approach which insists on acknowledgment of the primacy of conscience in interpretation actually allows for a fuller appreciation of the Bible, certainly a better appreciation of it than that which obtains in fundamentalism.

And what about the authority of the *ekklesia*, that is, its officers?

To make the *ekklesia* the final authority is to invite priestcraft. The church, properly, can only be a guide, an educator - and that is a lot. Its officers must recognize its limits as an earthly institution; the limits of its jurisdiction in this life (which include its inability to forecast anyone's destiny in the next). What group (or individual) is qualified to damn others to hell, annihilation or any such thing?

Society has laws; let the law rule our earthly affairs. This does not mean there is no place for the church and other religious institutions. These will always have a role in informing the law. The separation of religion and state can only be approximated; it is never absolute.

Chapter Six
Respecting God's Word: its limits included

In the previous chapter I suggested that conscience (alternately called the New Covenant, the Logos, Ma'at and so on) is a divine-human phenomenon reflecting the essential oneness or unity of God and man.

I also suggested that the fundamentalist idealistic exaltation of the Bible as an inerrant and infallible guide and the corresponding devaluation of the role and function of conscience is the result of an inability or refusal to accept such a proposition.

However, it seems to me that passages like the first part of 1 John 3:1 point precisely in a "divine-human" direction;

> Behold, what manner of love the Father hath
> bestowed upon us, that we should be called the sons of
> God:

verse 2 strengthens this view, as it declares,

> Beloved, now are we the sons of God, and it doth not
> yet appear what we shall be: but we know that, when he
> shall appear, we shall be like him; for we shall see him as
> he is.

Then there is 2 Corinthians 3:18 which according to the Amplified Bible speaks of believers being transformed into God's very own image.

> And all of us, as with unveiled face, [because we]
> continued to behold [in the Word of God] as in a mirror
> the glory of God, are constantly being transfigured into
> His very own image in ever increasing splendour and
> from one degree of Glory to another; [for this comes]
> from the Lord [Who is] the Spirit.

I must say though that I think it is unfortunate that the Amplified Version of the Bible should suggest that the "mirror" into which we look and which facilitates our "transfiguration" is *scripture*. Given the Amplified Bible's fundamentalist orientation, I am assuming that the phrase "the Word of God" in that version's footnote is a reference to the Bible.

I prefer to see the "mirror" as a metaphor for the self-exploratory phenomenon that is conscience. After all, mirrors are used to examine *oneself*.

Certainly, the Bible and other scriptures can assist in the process of self-examination, but in the context of this entire chapter's anti-literalistic contrast between the law written on stone and that written in the heart (the New Covenant), this passage seems to point to a more inward, spiritual investigation.

Coincidentally, this "mirror" imagery also recalls the profoundly spiritual "I and I" formulae of the Rastafarian faith, which I must confess, I find peculiarly attractive because of my Afro-Caribbean heritage.

I should also say though that I am somewhat concerned about the literalistic posture of some strains of Rastafarianism, especially their acceptance of fundamentalist ideas about the Bible - its inspiration, reliability and so on. But back to the point at hand.

That the Bible supports the view that God and man are one, a unity - is borne out especially in the proposition of the incarnation.

The incarnation, the suggestion that the man Jesus of Nazareth was God in the flesh, is a key tenet of Christian teaching. This is the "Mystery of Godliness" (1Timothy 3:16) which arguably, the vast majority of Christians embrace.

Yet traditionally, the same Christians shrink from the idea that humanity is now or ever can be partakers of divinity. An interesting article on anthropomorphisms (manifestations or depictions of God in human terms) in ISBE[1] is careful to note that this type of biblical language sets man the end-of-time goal,

> ...not of divinization but of assumption to eternal sonship...

But is not the Son of mainstream Christianity a part of the one reality that is called the Triune God? What then is the difference between his sonship and that which the elect are destined, or as some traditions teach, predestined to assume? What is the difference?

In 1Peter 2:24 it is said that he bore our sins "to the tree" (not on the tree, as in the King James Version). At what point did he take them on him? The bearing of our sins did not occur as Jesus hung on the cross but some time prior.

Some say he took them on in the garden of Gethsemane but why stop there? Was he not slain from the foundation of the world (Revelation 13:8)? Is it not conceivable that he carried our sins from his conception? Just whose virginity is the doctrine of the immaculate conception preserving? I mean no irreverence here.

And what about the mode of carriage, the manner in which Jesus is said to have carried our sins? Was it a detached conveyance, the manner in which one bears a burden on one's back or shoulders? Or is it as the scribe of 1Peter 2:24 suggests, that he bore our sins "in his own body"?

Another writer declared that he was "made" sin: the sinless virtually made sinful. It seems to me that our sins may be as much his, as his righteousness is claimed to be ours.

You will say our sins were imputed to him. Was our humanity in him merely a matter of imputation? Did he not die as humanity dies, from the foundation of the world? Perhaps the mystery of Godliness is no greater than the mystery of humanity.

I have to confess that this latter mystery is the one which most engages my attention. I am fascinated by the paradoxes, anomalies and "antimonies" of human nature. These can be just as insoluble as the mysteries of God.

I may never resolve the fundamental questions regarding God and the universe, at least not at a conscious level: I understand a significant percentage of the human brain's activity is unconscious.

Yet I feel that if I have some success at the human level - if for example, I can at least breach some of the gaps that exist between my own consciousness and that of others, if I can at least see past barriers like language, race and religion and somehow empathize, somehow "conscience" through others' eyes - I may indirectly, maybe inadvertently satisfy the "Divine Will".

In an attempt to grapple with the "problems" of the fundamentalist concept of inspiration fundamentalist theologian J.I. Packer suggests, albeit tentatively, that the mystery of the inspiration may be resolved in terms of what he calls a divine concursus - a coaction of God and man (Eerdman Bible Commentary).

I have reached the resolve that my greatest duty is to love myself and fellow humans whom I see, at least as much as I love God, whom I cannot see - but for myself and fellow humans, who bear the image of God no less than his word in our consciences.

This is how I reached that resolve, initially.

It was 1988 and I was caught in the throes of fundamentalist disillusionment. I had withdrawn from my local church for the first time[2] and sensed a need for Christian companionship.

I had some friends who were members of the interdenominational group Graduate Ministries Christian Fellowship[3], so I began to spend a lot of time with that group.

At my friends' invitation, I accompanied this group to the island of St. Vincent, where they were going on a weekend missionary and recreational trip. It was on the final day of this retreat, that my friends and I narrowly escaped what seemed like certain death.

We had taken a boat ride to Bequia, one of the smaller islands off St. Vincent. The journey across has a reputation for being turbulent, but we made it with relative ease, the first time. It was on the return trip that our faith was tested.

I was in the single cabin of the vessel when the trouble started. I was lying on a wooden bunk and noticed that the rocking of the boat was becoming increasingly violent. Soon it was impossible to remain lying down without risking some injury. I went up to the deck to see what was going on.

As I emerged, I was greeted by fierce wind and rain, swelling waves and the mostly frightened faces of my companions. There were a few worried smiles among my youthful peers, but soon even those would fade into panicked, sober or bewildered gazes, as the gravity of our situation sunk home.

The boat we were on must have been at least 20 feet long, but the raging waves made it seem like a little paper boat - tossing it up in the air, and then rising in a huge, threatening mass of dark waves around us as we came crashing down.

That was the scariest part, this drop through midair: your stomach contracted with the suspense, and this was followed by a loud crash into the churning sea. It seemed as though the waves would devour us.

Reflecting on that experience now, I seem to recall moments when I could not see the sky, and was even inclined to wonder which direction it was in, for it seemed almost as though the boat was somersaulting. I guess the trauma of our peril had us all a bit disoriented. It was difficult to tell which way was up.

Actually, a smaller docking vessel (about eight feet long) which we were towing with our supplies did overturn, doing nothing to allay our fears.

Peter Farnum, now with Youth With a Mission, but then the leader of our group, had raised a few choruses to try to hearten us but that was soon overtaken by crying and screaming, vomiting, and prayers for deliverance. Some people were fainting. One young lady fainted at least twice, repeatedly overwhelmed by our grim reality.

There we were, caught in a storm, being tossed defenselessly by the waves. And this was as true of my frame of mind as it was of our physical situation. Remember, these were the days of my disillusionment. Much of the time I was in a stupor, adrift on a sea of uncertainty. I had lost the sense of calm assurance, the sense of sins forgiven and fundamental purposefulness, that I once enjoyed. I was not confident (as I believe most of the others were) that should the boat capsize and I be taken via a watery death to the throne of judgment, that God would look on me favourably.

This was my preoccupation. More than a painful death by drowning, I feared for my soul's destiny. I could not pray with any sense of security. I felt only anxiety and presentiment. What could I say to God at this fateful moment, in this state of unbelief?

Then I remembered a simple principle that I had resolved to live by long ago, probably as a child. I would be honest with God. I would level with the Almighty, and tell him exactly where I stood and what I was feeling. This I thought was the best I could do.

My "prayer", an unspoken discourse, went something like this:

> Well, Lord, look me here; I ain't saying no pious
> prayer, 'cause I don't believe that make sense now. You
> know what I have been going through, and you know

where I stand. It don't make no sense trying to hide anything from you 'cause I know you can see my heart. If I die out here today, I don't know whether I am going to heaven or hell. I am not even sure that I believe in such places anymore.

Lord, I am leaving it up to you. Whatever you do with me is well done. I am confident that you will do what in your wisdom, is best. As for me, I taking a look around this boat and see what I can hold-on to when it falls apart. That may be my only chance of coming out of this alive. What lies beyond death is out of my control. I will do what I can for myself in this life.

This prayer did not calm the waves around me, but it made me feel better on the inside. I felt a sense of peace and composure. I was even able to comfort a dear friend in the group. She would later say she did not know what she would have done if I had not been there.

There was no irreverence in my prayer. Just the admission that as far as preparing for eternity was concerned, I had come to the end of myself. I had no answers. God would have to dispose of me as He saw fit. I reasoned that if God felt that I deserved to go to hell then He would know why, and that was enough for me. My part was just to be honest with myself. I felt God already knew what was in my heart. The important thing for me was not to lie to myself: I needed to have a clear conscience.

This "theology" may seem crude, even primitive, but at the end of all my investigation and exegesis of the Bible, church-history and (to a lesser extent) other religions, it is all I have. And quite frankly, it is enough for me.

There is another paradox here. It seems that the more we find out about God, the more conscious we become of how little we really know about him...or her.

I have come to the conclusion that this is a good place to be at. We can appreciate the Bible most soundly here. I am convinced that the greatest profits to be derived from scripture are bound up in an appreciation of its limits in communicating God's truth.

I leave you with these words of humanitarian Dr. Stan Mooneyham, taken from his book Travelling Hopefully[4]. If I am not mistaken he has been a champion of the evangelical cause, and so the agreement of our views is something of a mystery (yes, another one) to me.

> ...I am absolutely certain of fewer things, but of the things that remain, I am more certain than ever before...Now I affirm people more and my convictions less...

NOTES

Introduction

1. See "Church" in the International Standard Bible Encyclopaedia.

2. I once made some inquiries about the level of accountability in these churches in Barbados via an informal telephone survey. In one case, a church executive informed me that the leaders of her assembly (presumably including herself) did not discuss the church's finances with the congregation because the congregation has no business enquiring into such matters. She felt the church's budget was under the pastor's jurisdiction only. The Pastor was her husband.
I published the results of that survey in a booklet on this subject entitled "The Accountability Crisis in Caribbean Churches".

3. Richard Carter; Study of the causes and effects of urban migration in Barbados, 1992.

4. Preface; SCM Press Ltd 1984, 26-30 Tottenham Road, London N1.

5. The International Standard Bible Encyclopaedia (vol. I 1979, vol. II 1982, vol. III 1986, vol. VI 1988).

6. DOUBT, Wycliffe Bible Encyclopaedia.

7. P. 646-647 The History of Christianity (THC).

8. P. 485 THC

Ch 1. The nature and scope of the problem elaborated

1. See INTERPRETATION, HISTORY OF, ISBE.

2. I am thinking here of clerics within the older churches who are always prepared to give the church fathers the benefit of the doubt. I usually try to temper my judgments with the same principle, but in this case I find it difficult to resist the conclusion that some of the church fathers intended to make the Bible an object of obedience-inducing fear.

3. For example, the "inerrancy and infallibility" of scripture is implied by such writers as Origen, Basil and Jerome. ISBE notes that among these writers

> Inspiration is seen as applying equally to every book and to scripture as a whole. All its writers were moved by the same Spirit and everything they wrote, including such details as lists of names, must be regarded as inspired reliable and profitable.

It is also noted that Augustine defined inspiration as "..a stimulation and control that would rule out mistakes."

4. This perception of scripture tends to equate it with God.

5. Interpreter's Dictionary of the Bible, Abingdon Press 1989.

6. Idols and the Church Universal, pp 26, 27 Caribbean Week, March 2-15 1996.

7. See pp 178,179 in Escaping From Fundamentalism.

8. I prefer to call him Joshua myself since this is the correct English translation of the Greek *Iesous*: "Jesus" is merely a transliteration of the Greek name. In its article ENGLISH VERSIONS (V. Authorized or King James Version), ISBE comments that the use of "Jesus" instead of Joshua represents a "particularly bad example" of

the King James translators failure to abide by one of the rules that were supposed to govern their work - specifically, that biblical names should correspond to popular usage and there should be no attempt to follow the Hebrew or Greek so closely as the Geneva and Bishop's bibles had done.

9. see George Fox and the Quakers, p. 500, THC.

10. see Jesus Christ, A. 4. Is a life of Jesus possible, IDB.

11. Jesus Christ, A. 2., IDB.

12. I am inclined to use the masculine gender pronoun because of convenience and habit. However I am not opposed to the view that the feminine pronoun may be used when referring to God. In fact I think it is significant that the first real representations of a deity were female figurines. See The World's Religions, pp 25-27.

Ch 2. Examining the Fundamentalist Doctrine of the Inerrancy and Infallibility of the Bible.

1. See BIBLE, 1. A., ISBE.

2. "Septuagint" (abbreviated LXX) is the name commonly applied to the Greek version of the Jewish scriptures most widely used in antiquity. It is this text, not the Hebrew scriptures, which is quoted by the "New Testament" writers.

3. The error of the Septuagint that I am referring to here is the use of the Greek *diatheke*, meaning "a will or testament", to translate the Hebrew *berit* which means "a covenant". This was an unfortunate error because the use of *diatheke* and the consequent definition of the Jewish and Christian dispensations by the term "Testament" (Old and New) detracts from the very essence of the covenant idea - the essence of *berit*. This is because, *berit* signifies "that which binds two parties together: the agreement itself, not the symbols, code, treaty or any

other written stipulations associated with it - under which category *diatheke* falls. *Berit* brings into focus the internally oriented essence of the covenant "bond", not the external, literal or tangible phenomenon associated with it.

Commenting on the concept of the *berit* in the ancient Near East, ISBE (Covenant [OT]) points out that

> In every case...the bond between the parties was wider than the mere treaty obligations...

Berit therefore focuses less on words and more on their meaning, that is, the intentions in the hearts of the parties to the covenant. I repeatedly emphasize the difference between words and meaning in this book.

The church-fathers' erroneous identification of the Jewish and Christian scriptures as "Testaments" (which was encouraged by the use of *diatheke* in the Septuagint) has compounded the problem. To clarify the issue, the reader is advised to note that the Jewish scriptures do not include any material that could be properly called a testament. However, these scriptures include records of a number of covenants (e.g. the Noahic, Abrahamic, Davidic and Sinaitic covenants), but only with some difficulty can it be described collectively as a single covenant.

The reader may note too that the inappropriateness of *diatheke* to translate *berit* is also underscored by the fact that wills (testaments) were not common in Jewish culture (COVENANT [NT], ISBE).

4. See INSPIRATION, II. Relevant Passages, ISBE.

5. EFF p 3.

6. See INFALLIBILITY, ISBE.

7. The legalistic posture of passages like Matthew 5:17 for example, is well known.

8. See "committed", The Complete Word Study Dictionary, New Testament, 1992 AMG Publishers.

9. See GOSPEL, I. Derivation of the Term, ISBE.

10. Luke 1:2.

11. See TRADITION, I. General Remarks, ISBE.

12.Pg. 5, EFF.

13. This appears to have been an oversight on Barr's part. I have pointed out that the use of the phrase *te gramma* identifies the scriptures referred to as the sacred texts of Judaism.

14. See remarks on this passage in Eerdmans New Bible Commentary.

Ch. 3 The True Basis of Fundamentalism.

i) The influence of legalistic Judaism.

1. A common name by which Jewish opponents of Jesus identified him.

2. See TORAH. II. B., ISBE.

3. See Jesus Christ. A. 2. h., IDB.

4. See TORAH. II. C. ISBE.

5. see APOCRYPHAL GOSPELS. IV. A., ISBE.
6. E.F.F, pg 14

ii) The introduction and establishment of the ekklesia.

1. Christian Literature Crusade.

2. Jesus Christ. A. Sources 2. h., The question of Authenticity, IDB.

3. For example, Matthew 4:23; 5:3, 10, 19, 20; 6:10, 33; Mark 1:14; 4:11, 26, 30; Luke 4:43; 8:1,10; 9:2; John 3:3, 5.

4. Jesus Christ. E. 3., The message of the kingdom of God, IDB.

5. See "Church" ISBE and "CHURCH, IDEA OF" IDB.

6. See Paul the apostle, a. The meaning of the Church, IDB.

7. CHURCH, Origin of the Term, Wycliffe Bible Encyclopedia.

8. Jesus Christ. E. 3. e. Was the kingdom identical with the church, IDB.

9. The activities of this assembly of Jewish religious leaders is disputed, but the evidence points conclusively to the fact that such an assembly was convened under Rabbi Johanan ben Zakki toward the end of the first century. Also beyond dispute is the addition of a nineteenth "benediction", to the Eighteen Benedictions (also called the Tefillah) of Jewish synagogue worship. This "benediction", the birkat haminim ("blessing [=cursing] of the apostates"), attributed to Simon the Little, was added at the direction of Rabban Gamaliel II. The wording of this "blessing" has changed several times, but it has been suggested that in its earliest form, it may have read "For apostates may there be no hope, and may the Nazarenes and the heretics suddenly perish". That it was originally intended for Christians is hinted at in this modern reading which refers to the arrogant "kingdom":

> For slanderers, let there be no hope. May all wickedness quickly perish. May all your enemies be cut off. May you speedily uproot the arrogant kingdom, and break it, crush it, and humble it speedily in our days. Blessed are you, O Lord, who breaks the enemies and humbles the arrogant.

See SYNAGOGUE, V. B.,CANON OF THE OT, II. D. 3, and RELIGIONS: JUDAISM, II.

D. 2. Christianity as a Sect, ISBE.
THC also refers to the inclusion of these "blessings" in the Jews synagogue worship; see Preaching and Public argument, Pg. 78.

10. For example by IDB; see Congregation.

11. There are some things which may be referred to as being "among us", (that is, things we have in common) which are not externally oriented phenomena, e.g. conscience.

12. As shall be seen in section iv of this chapter, I am of the opinion that the gains made during the Reformation have been overrated and that this movement has significantly reinforced the terror of the Bible.

13. The World's Religions, 1991, Lion Publishing plc.

14. Pg. 32; Fount Paperbacks September 1977, twenty-seventh impression August 1986.

iii) The creation of a distinctly Christian canon.

1. Canon of the NT, III. B. 1. ISBE.

2. See footnote 1.
3. See CANON OF THE OT, ISBE.

4. Pg. 64 of this text.

5. Pg. 101 THC

6. See HERESY, I, II and III, ISBE.

iv) The error of the Reformers.

1. The theory of the different levels of meaning in scripture was introduced by Origen. The fourfold interpretation was most popular, but at times as many as seven levels were cited. See

138

INTERPRETATION, HISTORY OF, IV. C. Middle Ages, ISBE.

2. INTERPRETATION, HISTORY OF, IV. D. Reformation, ISBE.

3. P 173, EFF.

4. P 13 EFF.

Ch. 4 The New Covenant.

1. The New Covenant principle is basically about individual (personal) faith and responsibility and hence God's concern with the intent of the heart, rather than outward appearances. Less explicit references to this principle include the story of David's selection as Israel's king in 1 Samuel 16, especially verse 7, and Ezekiel's declaration of God's intention to judge Israel on an individual basis (Ezekiel 18).

2. Case-histories, pg. 34, The World's Religions.

3. Pg. 95

4. Priestcraft and magic, pg. 38, The World's Religions.

5. Ritual, pg. 37, The World's Religions.

6. Brow mentions "the emergence of the vast system of medieval priestcraft within Christendom" (pg. 39). It is my view that Christianity has borne the stamp of priestcraft from its formative years, that is, for as long as the *ekklesia* has been its focus.

7. Pg. 80, The World's Religions; Religions of the biblical world: Persia, ISBE.

8. See footnote seven.

9. Pg.357, The World's Religions.

10. See Logos, Wycliffe Bible Encyclopaedia.

11. PHILO JUDAEUS, ISBE.

12. Pg. 109, The meaning of the faith, THC.

13. CONSCIENCE, 1. B. and C. ISBE

14. CONSCIENCE, II. B. ISBE

15. CONSCIENCE, II. A. ISBE

16. WISDOM, I . ISBE

Ch. 5 Conscience Vindicated

1. Merlene Cuthbert and Michael Pidgeon; Cedar Press, 1979. This text in particular makes a very poignant observation when it notes that the subjectivity and consequent obscurity of human language makes misunderstandings in communication between two persons speaking *the same* language more likely than two persons speaking different languages.

2. 1991, Macmillan Education Company.

3. This is a program through which the Caribbean Conference of Churches seeks to sensitize Christians to the need for an awareness of their social responsibility - especially toward the poor.

4. SIN, 1, ISBE

5. See footnote 16 of chapter 4.

Ch. 6 Respecting God's Word: its limits included

1. ANTHROPOMORPHISMS, V, ISBE

2. See introduction, pg. 7

3. This group had arisen out of the Interschool Christian Fellowship of Barbados.

4. pg. 9; 1984, Word Incorporated.

Bibliography

Eerdman New Bible Commentary

Escaping From Fundamentalism
James Barr 1984
SCM Press Ltd.

The Amplified Bible.
Zondervan Bible Publishers, 1965

The Complete Word Study Dictionary - New Testament.
AMG Publishers, 1992

The Four Loves, Fount Paperbacks 1986

The History of Christianity
Lion Publishing, 1990.

The International Standard Bible Encyclopaedia
William B. Eerdman's Publishing Co.
1979-1988 (four volumes).

The Interpreter's Dictionary of The Bible
Abingdon Press, 1989 (17th printing).

The World's Religions
Lion Publishing plc, 1991.

The Wycliffe Bible Commentary
The Moody Bible Institute of Chicago, 1962.

The Wycliffe Bible Encyclopaedia,
The Moody Bible Institute of Chicago, 1975.

Travelling Hopefully
Word Incorporated, 1984

About Junior (Jay) Campbell

"You give up too easily," my friend John Leach once said. We were adolescents then and as teenage lads, were keen on the occasional test of strength. "Larry", as we called him, was commenting on the brevity of my resistance during a pushing match he had just won. His words struck a note with me: I recognized the truth of them immediately. I also recognized I could do much better and resolved never to quit so easily again.

The publication of this book, seventeen years after it was originally written, and in defiance of extraordinary opposition, is just one by-product of that resolve. Another is the tenacity of thought that characterizes the organization I founded in my native Barbados, Intelek International (www.intelek.net). This tenacity is key to my work as a *holistic* communications and education specialist.

My tenacity powers the creativity that led one feminist poet to label me "a truly original thinker". It is the reason why I may even be credited by some Barbadians as having played a catalytic role in that island's contemporary cultural renaissance, and a similar regeneration in the arts, academia and politics throughout the Americas. I am not suggesting that I am famous: merely, that I have been effective.

Indeed, while my effectiveness may be one of Barbados' best kept secrets, my tenacity may have brought me some infamy. Some critics manage to equate it with unbridled self-interest or arrogance.

In 2002, British anti-terror authorities may even have confused *stick-to-it-iveness* with militant religious fervor. That year, on my first visit to England, I apparently came under their surveillance. Among other things, I was asked if I had ever been to Afghanistan and had I met Osama Bin Ladin.

Most people though – and I like to think some at MI5 and MI 6 are among them now – know that I am a tried and true advocate of non-violent conflict resolution. They know me as the promoter of "Poetic

Jazztice" – an artist committed to the triumph of virtue over vice: the authentic reconciliation of terror to beauty.

About Intelek International

Overview

With the help of a few friends, I founded Intelek International in Barbados in 1992. It was then called **Roots Academy** (RA).

The name "Roots Academy" reflected my focus on the things that humanity's varied knowledge systems have in common. Motivated by the experience that brought my book, **The Bible: Beauty and Terror Reconciled** into being, I was especially keen to not only highlight those things that are common to differing religious systems (like Christianity and Islam) but also the remarkable similarities and overlaps between secular scientific and religious faith-based ways of knowing.

This vision inspired RA's Statement of Agreement:

> *Because we believe in holistic education, that is, education which is comprehensive and caters to the whole person:*
>
> *1.As a means of promoting balanced self-respect or self-consciousness (recognition of one's potential and limitations) and a corresponding regard for others,*
>
> *2. As a means of promoting mutual understanding, tolerance and goodwill in society, and*
>
> *3. As a prerequisite for productive living - a stimulus to creativity, thrift and industry,*
>
> *We are resolved to work together for the advancement of such education through this organization, the Roots Academy.*

Goals

"To encourage good social relations among persons of diverse cultures and beliefs, by informing them of and emphasizing that which is common in their origins - their roots.

To encourage and facilitate the flourishing of diverse cultures (artistic expression etc) in an atmosphere of understanding and tolerance.

To co-operate with and assist other like-minded groups in the pursuit of common objectives.

Intelek's vision of holistic knowledge, intellectual honesty or the persistent pursuit of truth, flows naturally from my recognition of the importance of honesty with oneself - the necessity and validity of sustained individualistic, rational inquiry.

In the language of contemporary education theory and practice, you could say Intelek reflects my recognition of the importance of lifelong learning. This is at least part of what is meant by *holistic education,* as used in RA's Statement of Agreement.

Intelek also builds on my recognition of the inevitable diversity of human beliefs and opinions. In TBBTR, I celebrate diversity of faith and opinion, seeing it as an inescapable conclusion of honest learning, and an indicator of the necessity and value of tolerance.

Reflecting my own experience, Intelek's purpose could easily be stated in the same language and context of Christian and other religious ideals. However, like TBBTR, Intelek's appeals and challenges transcend religious terminology, labels and boundaries. The Intelek message of Informed Faith (the title of one of my earliest post-fundamentalist essays) and the necessity of tolerance, is directed to the Rastafarian, Christian, Jew, Hindu, Muslim, Bahai, Bhuddist and atheist alike. It speaks to both the capitalist and communist, as it addresses universal human strengths and weaknesses; it responds to universal needs and truths.

Also, while Intelek's objective is principally one of providing information and inspiration, it has always also been one of "action". The idea is not only to inspire individuals (primarily, but also groups) to the highest ideals, but also to help them bridge the gap between ideology and action; the gap between academics and the "real world".

I believe this gap is created and/or sustained by, among other things, persistent superficial distinctions between secular and religious education and activity.

What's in a name?

Contrary to the suggestion of prominent Barbadian radio journalist David Ellis, who launched an on-air attack on myself and Intelek in March 2002, I did not choose the name "Intelek" to suggest that I am more intelligent than anyone else. Rather, as the unconventional spelling of the word suggests, "Intelek" was intended to encourage Barbadians and others to *rethink* the very notion of "intelligence".

Particularly, my goal is to help people see intelligence as a phenomenon that manifests itself in a variety of ways across different countries, cultures, languages, races and other possible dividing lines. It seems to me that if there is one claim that we can safely make about the complex thing we call "human intelligence" it is that it can be expressed in very diverse manners.

147

I therefore chose the name "Intelek", a Bajanized (Barbadianized), phonetic representation of the Standard English word, first and foremost because of its ability to communicate a relaxed, unconventional understanding of the notion of intelligence.

While valuing and addressing the cognitive features of intelligence - the kind of knowledge that tends to dominate formal education systems - Intelek is particularly concerned with the affective factors that influence how we learn. Intelek focuses on attitudinal and emotional development, exploring the link between this development and our socialisation.

Fundamentally, Intelek emphasizes human interdependence. The Intelek slogan "For All We Know" is not simply intended to prompt the usual association of those words with the limits of human intelligence: it is not only suggesting there is more to learn collectively as the human race. Rather, it is declaring that there is room for all forms of knowledge among humanity.

Rejecting dogmatic secular scientific or religious claims to a monopoly on "true or factual" knowledge, Intelek advances a vision of knowledge that is "unified" in spite of our different understandings of what it is possible to know.

Intelek's evolving structure and associations

Intelek, then called Roots Academy (RA) was first registered as a charitable Trust in Barbados in 1994 (www.caipo.gov.bb/search/search_results.php#). Barbadian historian Trevor Marshall, psychiatrist Dr. Richard Corbin, and Jocelyn Clarke, then a bright young actuary with the former Barbados Mutual, now **Sagicor**, were the first Trustees.

Conrad Mason of the Caribbean Conference of Churches, then based in Barbados, also made a significant input at this initial stage. Mason's attitude was encouraging, overall, but he was nonetheless critical, especially of the brevity of the Statement of Agreement that I had put together. I had proposed that RA be initially founded on the Statement, perhaps in lieu of, or pending the later development of a constitution.

Dr. Corbin supported the Statement, noting particularly that its brevity would allow RA to be more open and inclusive in its membership and outreach initially. He thus assisted me in overcoming Mason's objections, and I regard that confidence boosting endorsement as his most important contribution to Intelek.

The contribution of entrepreneur David Harvey is harder to isolate. His enduring moral and practical support for me and RA, early on, and then Intelek, spanned several years and was invaluable.

David was a former Wesleyan when we met, and like I, had become disillusioned with fundamentalist Christianity. A tireless entrepreneurial enthusiast, he and I experimented with a number of growth models and strategies for Intelek. We both favoured the network selling model.

Stephen Massiah, a former member with me of the People's Cathedral - Barbados' largest and most prominent Pentecostal church was also helpful. Like Harvey, he too became a trustee of Intelek, when Clarke, Corbin and Marshall had moved on.

In 2002 Massiah played a key role in the publication of Viola Davis' book, "The Creative Use of Schizophrenia in Caribbean Writing", arguably Intelek's most ambitious publishing project up to that time.

Compared to the other relationships mentioned so far, Intelek's association with Davis, dating back to 1999 is rather recent (although she was one of my lecturers at the Barbados Community College in

1983). Still, as I suggest in the on-line introduction to Intelek's, my ongoing association with this distinguished Pan Africanist, educator, feminist and political activist, has been important to Intelek for a number of reasons

Stephen Mendes, a former Berean Christian, with close ties to Barbados' Jewish community also supported Intelek for a number of years. His company, Mendes Computers hosted the Intelek website, at a concessionary rate, up until 2008.

Though intermittent, the moral and practical support of graphic artist Andrew Skeete, feminist poet Margaret Gill, Anglican priest Dr. Leslie Lett and international education consultant Isaac Goodine was also very valuable.

Goodine, a Canadian diplomat and international education consultant then based in Barbados in the 1990s, was attracted to RA by some publicity I did for the organization in the **Barbados Advocate** newspaper, when I first registered it with the local Department of Corporate Affairs.

As I recall, Isaac was intrigued by the notion of holistic education I articulated, and especially by my understanding that this type of education both required and could bring about a *paradigm shift* in society's perceptions. Like I, he remains very enthusiastic about the notion of challenging existing paradigms or ways of viewing the world. He typically speaks of the "Aha" moment that individuals have, when they experience a paradigm shift in some aspect of their understanding of the world.

Despite bitter betrayals and disappointments dealt him by unscrupulous leaders of business in the Caribbean, Goodine remains committed to the advancement of holistic education in that region, as in Canada, where he is currently based, and elsewhere. He remains a staunch supporter of my efforts through Intelek and is expected to play a leading role in upcoming projects.

Intelek in the UK

Since moving to Norfolk in the UK in 2006, I have been exploring the various structural options that would allow me to continue and expand upon Intelek's work while I am here. I have been networking and collaborating with a number of NGO and business interests, including: the Sainsbury Centre for the Visual Arts (at the University of East Anglia), the Roman Catholic Justice and Peace Commission of Norwich, the Ihsan Mosque Muslim community of Norwich, Rainbow Nations, the Norfolk and Norwich Racial Equality Council, Domino's Pizza and others.

In October 2007, I teamed-up with members of the Ihsan Mosque and the Roman Catholic Church of St. John the Baptist to coordinate a fundraising inter-faith football match, under the Spirited Sport label launched by Intelek in Barbados. I have also led a number of diversity and conflict resolution workshops in schools around Norfolk and Suffolk, through my affiliation with Rainbow Nations, a Community Interest Company (CIC).

I find the CIC model somewhat attractive, but my experience with Rainbow Nations has suggested that this structure can be rather unwieldy. So for the time being, I am pursuing my holistic education and communications social agenda as a sole trader, and have registered Intelek International as the title under which I trade - to safeguard Intelek's continuity.

Intelek's work therefore continues apace, while organizational and/or structural matters are being resolved gradually - with the assistance of legal firm Gordon Dean Solicitors, business development consultants Bizz Fizz, Work House and similar Norwich-based agencies.

I anticipate that with the publication of TBBTR, the spread of Intelek's message will accelerate significantly.

Collaborations and partnerships between Intelek and internet based agencies and interests like Facebook, the Institute for Global Church Studies (www.igcsforum.org) and Allvoices (www.allvoices.com) are expected to play a significant role in this acceleration. This is in keeping with Intelek's people empowering Creole Complementarity Interactive Technology vision, which capitalizes on social networking (see below).

Intelek's
Creole Complementarity Interactive Technology

The paradox of the "communication age" is that there is
so little authentic communication happening; so little
empathy, genuine sharing and understanding; so little
collectivity. There is an *excessively* capitalistic, 'copy-
cat', mechanized, mass production dimension to modern
communication which is inhibiting authentic, internal
processing and retention of information: a mechanized,
mass production dimension to modern education that is
inhibiting authentic learning. (From the original CCIT
introductory essay, 2002)

Intelek's **Creole Complementarity Interactive Technology** (CCIT,
pronounced "sit") can be thought of as a holistic, *edupreneurial*
initiative. A fundamental aim of CCIT is to combine earning and
learning in an exciting organic, dynamic and deeply fulfilling manner.

You can simply purchase a hardcopy of TBBTR for £14.00
(US$21.25), approx.) or any other Intelek product or service at an
agreed price, for your own private, personal use.

Or, you can join Intelek's CCIT journey, and become an authorized
distributor of these products and services. This may be a particularly
attractive option now, for persons looking for employment or
struggling to make ends meet during the current global economic
crisis.

Intelek offers very generous commissions - for example £6 on each
sale of a hardcopy of TBBTR.

The most exciting aspect of Intelek's CCIT though, is the opportunity it provides for you to capitalize on your own intellectual property. Yes, Intelek will help you tell your own story. You might be surprised to find that it intersects with Intelek's in significant ways.

Martin Luther King Jr. has said:

> In a real sense all life is inter-related. All men are caught in an inescapable network of mutuality, tied in a single garment of destiny. Whatever affects one directly affects all indirectly. I can never be what I ought to be until you are what you ought to be, and you can never be what you ought to be until I am what I ought to be. This is the inter-related structure of reality.

One of the goals of Intelek's CCIT is to facilitate "thought tracking" - that is, to trace the transmission and development of ideas around the world. You might be surprised to learn how your thoughts, words or deeds have touched the lives of others. Think about the **butterfly effect**.

I am particularly keen to prove (or disprove, with equal enthusiasm) my own theory that ideas I first outlined in TBBTR about sixteen years ago have been circulated around the globe and have made a significant contribution to the current world-wide renaissance in religious and secular knowledge systems.

The following background and related information will give you a sense of how this could be.

It will also help you to appreciate the regulations that govern the legally binding covenants that Intelek establishes with authorised distributors, as these are rooted in the sense of responsibility I feel for the impact my intellectual labours have on others.

Background

I first embarked on Intelek's Creole Complementarity Interactive Technology project about eight years ago, in Barbados. An essentially interactive, holistic education and broader publishing strategy, the

154

idea for CCIT evolved in response to financial and pedagogical (practical teaching) challenges that had prevented me from publishing TBBTR in the 1990s.

The financial challenges centered on the cost of printing TBBTR. The book is approximately 150 pages in length. All the other publications I had produced up to that time - two comic books, three collections of poetry, a couple religious tracts, and so on - were about 50 pages or less.

I had basically finished writing TBBTR (except for a few small modifications) in 1994 or so, but by 2002 I had been prevented from publishing it by the prohibitive cost of printing a book that size in sufficient quantities to make the venture financially viable.

Another, at *least* equally important reason for my failure to publish TBBTR up to 2002 was my concern that the book might be used by individuals or groups in a way I had not intended. I was concerned that it might become an object of the same kind of religious or broader ideological abuse that it was intended to prevent: the kind of abuse that the inflexible, intimidating fundamentalist evangelical Christian interpretation of the Bible is known for.

The related possibility of copyright infringement was also a factor in my thinking. That was secondary though. My primary concern was more *fundamental*, stemming from the "quieted trauma" I had undergone as my investigation into the history of the Bible, the church and religion generally, led me to an extraordinary awareness of the extent to which so-called *fundamentalist* Christianity - the belief system to which I had surrendered myself unconditionally - had become corrupted and shallow almost from its very inception!

It is clear to me now that while the cost of printing TBBTR was certainly a reason behind the delay in getting the book out, an equally or more significant reason was my desire to spare others the kind of trauma I had undergone in coming to terms with the shallow character of the faith on which I had been basing all my life's ambitions.

I had thought of publishing TBBTR on floppy or compact discs before, to get around the printing costs, but the CCIT concept was born when I came up with the idea of employing a system of bespoke or personalized covenant-making between myself and customers buying the book in electronic form.

This notion of fusing electronic technology with fleshy, face-to-face or one-to-one, time honoured methods of human communication, commerce and commitment is essentially what CCIT is about.

The concept can also be traced back to my booklet "The Word Becomes Flesh" (TWBF), first published in Barbados in 2001, to commemorate the United Nations' World Conference Against Racism, Racial Discrimination, Xenophobia and Related forms of Intolerance (WCAR). I had hoped to re-publish TWBF again in 2009, along with an online book project, to commemorate a UN follow-up to WCAR, the **Durban Review Conference**, held in Geneva.

In TWBF, I seek to alert readers to the mass production mode of knowledge transmission that the advent of the printing press (thanks Gutenberg!) has facilitated. There I suggest that:

> The accelerated acquisition of knowledge that many hail as the greatest achievement of the modern world has cost, and continues to cost humanity at a tremendous price: the institutionalization and intensification of prejudices, especially Euro-American prejudices.

TWBF acknowledges the many persons within the developed "Euro-American camp" who appreciate the hazards that attend the accelerated, lopsided "progress" of the Western world. (And it is probably worth noting here that if organic models of commerce such as those promoted by bartering societies in the USA and Europe were more widely practiced in these societies, humanity probably would not now be dealing with the current global financial crisis.)

Fundamentally, TWBF deplores the moral disconnect or disengagement - the failure of authentic experience - that limits authentic knowing or engagement in all realms, not only in the realms of economics or religion.

As I comment in a document written in 2008 to support the second edition of Viola Davis' book The Creative Use of Schizophrenia In Caribbean Writing (CUOS), published by Intelek in 2002, TWBF was my way of insisting that authenticity turns on the question of the human capacity for truth, rather than our schizophrenic secular-religious and other contests around "intelligence".

The original CCIT introductory essay which, incidentally, was published as an appendage to CUOS, reflects this concern. Indeed, this is fundamentally what CCIT is about: how our vision of the world and our values affect our capacity to learn (or teach). It is about how our honesty, or lack thereof, affects what we can "know": especially, what we can know about ourselves - who we *are*.

As I first stated in the promotional essay over seven years ago, CCIT

> ...encourages users to take the time, and space, necessary
> for personal reflection, and hence authentic learning. It
> encourages the quality of self-knowledge that is vital to
> active learner participation in and ownership of learning
> activity - rather than rote, mechanistic, superficial and
> fragmentary learning

I consider electronic publishing particularly useful in this regard, as unlike printed text, it can allow both intensive and extensive engagement with the text by the reader - copying, cutting and pasting text; highlighting sections of text through the bold and italic functions; colouring sections of text; increasing, decreasing and otherwise varying fonts, and so on. CCIT facilitates the *personalization* of the text in these and related manners. And this is to

157

say nothing of the obvious environmental advantages that result from less demand for paper.

Of course, this level of engagement with texts cannot exist in isolation from a propensity for authentic engagement generally: that is, it reflects the propensity or tendency of the reader to be authentically engaged - or *present* - in all aspects of his or her life.

The primary failing of fundamentalist Christianity - and other religious and secular ideological or knowledge systems is their propensity toward disengagement from reality: their propensity toward distraction from fundamental truth. As indicated above, a key theme of TBBTR, is the self-defeating tendency of fundamentalist religions to obscure fundamental truths.

Secular or so-called "scientific" forms of fundamentalism - as represented perhaps by Richard Dawkins, James Watson and other prominent intellectuals in the UK, the USA, the Caribbean and elsewhere - behave in the same way. The ivory tower tendencies of secular academic institutions and movements are as much a feature of such disengagement as the pie-in-the-sky pedagogy we associate with religious sermonizing.

At its core, the problem is at *least* as much a societal or cultural problem. It is not peculiar to any particular individual or group. Tara Brabazon, professor of media studies at Brighton University addressed this holistic character of the problem in a BBC interview.

Brabazon was one of a number of expert commentators featured on the March 19th, 2009 episode of the BBC Radio 4 flagship programme **Analysis**. Presented by the academic/activist Kenan Malik, the documentary entitled **Clever.com** explored issues around the impact of internet technology on the reading habits and intellectual attainment of persons growing up with the unfettered, often unfiltered access to information that the internet allows.

Malik, who seems to blame internet usage for an apparent deterioration in his own *mature* powers of concentration, seemed intent on blaming youthful academics' subscription to Facebook, You Tube and similar internet communication phenomena for their declining academic output. He seemed set to view their internet usage as a vindication of Brabazon's controversial banning of her students from using Google and Wikipedia.

However, Brabazon's rationale for that ban turned out to be rather more textured. She said:

> I would never blame the students. My students are not doing anything that the rest of us are not doing. I don't believe in phrases like the Google Generation and Digital Natives. I think the whole culture is engaging in very superficial searching. I think we're all like grazing information. Very few people are drilling down more deeply. So I think my students aren't doing anything unusual. We're all rewarded for being superficial, we're all rewarded for not digging too deeply, not making people uncomfortable, but what we have to do at university is challenge people and get people a bit uncomfortable and move out of their comfort zone.

I believe that it is such superficial searching, spread over approximately *2100 years*, that is responsible for the deeply degenerate state of shallow fundamentalist Christianity, Islam and other religious and secular belief and thought systems.

The goal of Intelek's CCIT is to help all people (not just university students) engage in a *penetrative* - passionate, yet focused, cohesive, concentrated and constructive way - with all forms of knowledge.

The Intelek vision stems from my belief that just as faith and reason are complementary, rather than antithetical or opposed to each other, passion and reason are also fundamentally complementary.

It is a fusion (or *creolization*) of passion and reason, at the very least, that has kept me focused on TBBTR, seeing the manuscript through to completion over a period of approximately seven years. The same fusion of passion and reason has enabled me to persevere for an additional sixteen years, to see TBBTR through to publication.

My heart's desire is to have others share in this experience: to see them fuse passion and reason in their own lives so that they too can realize their potential fully. This is partly what the Intelek slogan "For all we know" is about. The double helix symbol in the Intelek logo hints at my persistent, profound belief in humanity.

The first CCIT Covenants

One of the first persons I entered a CCIT covenant with was Elijah Marshall of the Sons of God Apostolic Church in Barbados. I may have the last name wrong, but I am sure it was *not* Williams - although this chap does resemble the head of his church - Arch Bishop Granville Williams - in significant ways.

I still remember the day he came to Poetpourri House, on Dalkeith Road in the parish of St. Michael - my home, in those days (it has been virtually under siege for a number of years now) and the cradle not only of Intelek International, but also the organization called Roots Academy, out of which Intelek has grown.

I remember Elijah standing next to me, as I typed up the terms of our agreement on my computer. When I asked him how much he could pay for the book, he said that he was almost broke. I had no reason to doubt him. Like I, at times given to dreaming, Elijah, seemed to be constantly struggling with his finances. A deeply spiritual man, consumed by a pious passion, he struggled to give his faith pragmatic expression in the materialistic minefield that is Barbados' social ethos.

I sold Elijah the book for a penny, or a similar nominal sum, to authenticate the transaction. He thanked me and said I was a great man. I thanked him for the kind compliment.

I think he understood what I was trying to achieve. I think he realized that my primary motivation is not the money I can make from TBBTR but the lessons I feel this book can teach.

My memory is a bit vague now, but I believe I also made similar CCIT covenants with my brother Wayne and my cousin Michelle. As far as I recall, no money was exchanged in these transactions.

So, while financial gain or viability has always been an important consideration where Intelek's CCIT is concerned, it has never been the primary consideration.

CCIT and the University of the West Indies

In 2002 I also sought to make an alliance between Intelek and the University of the West Indies (UWI), so that we could develop the CCIT concept together. I made approaches to the Barbados-based UWI Cave Hill Campus Principal, Professor Sir Hilary Beckles and Professor Mark Mckwat of the Department of Language and Linguistics. Unfortunately these approaches bore no fruit.

Professor Beckles had expressed great enthusiasm about TBBTR when he had read a draft of the text in 1994 or so. Actually, he and his colleague Dr. Alvin Thompson of UWI's History department were among the first persons I shared the document with.

However, by 2002 Beckles' enthusiasm for TBBTR had long faded and his response to my approach about CCIT was decidedly cold. The reasons for either situation still remain obscure to me, but I know that he is as much a politician, as he is an educator. I am also mindful of the observation made by former Barbados Prime Minister Sir Lloyd Erskine Sandiford, about the viciousness of academic politics.

CCIT falls into abeyance

With the passage of time, as I failed to get the support I was seeking to develop the CCIT concept, and as the obligations of married life and then fatherhood exacted increasing tolls on my energies and attention, Intelek's CCIT fell into abeyance.

The unspectacular performance of the two texts actually published around the time I first initiated Intelek's CCIT (TWBF and CUOS) was also probably a factor causing the loss of momentum.

Interestingly, it was my effort in 2008 to make good on my and Viola Davis' original vision for CUOS that led to the present revival of the CCIT project.

CCIT Now

The revival of Intelek's CCIT is off to a very promising start. Over the past four months or so I have been experimenting with various types of Covenants and assessing the feedback I have been receiving from potential purchasers and distributors of TBBTR and other Intelek books, Cds and similar materials.

The effort this time around has been significantly aided by the prevailing interest in "new expressions" of the Christian faith, and evidence in popular media of the public's readiness - or at least the readiness of persons shaping public opinion - to engage with issues surrounding Christianity in a radical, reformation-prioritizing manner.

The recent BBC TV Channel 4 series, Christianity: A History, and investigative, analytical challenges to the canonical gospels' account of the life of Jesus led by Anglican cleric Peter Owen-Jones, theologian Robert Beckford and others, have helped me to overcome the deep trauma-triggered reservations that kept me putting the publication of TBBTR on hold. I've come to think that perhaps,

162

despite my reluctance to do so back in 1991 or so, there was a part of me that agreed with Ian Weithers, an Anglican friend who told me the time for TBBTR had not yet come.

I believe it has now.

Of course, Intelek's CCIT is not just restricted to TBBTR. This dynamic, organic, evolving technology is being used to advance all of Intelek's programmes. Indeed, it may be viewed as simply a combination or consolidation of all of Intelek's efforts to advance the vision of holistic education.

Join the CCIT journey

To join the Intelek International CCIT journey, contact Intelek by email at poeticjazztice04@yahoo.co.uk or on 4407920 884 222.

You can also join the Intelek International group on Facebook.

Index

A

academic
   basis of author's views on conscience, 126
   greed, 7
academic institutions
   secular, 'ivory tower' tendencies, 173
academic politics
   minefield in Barbados, 6
   visciousness of, 176
academics
   and the real world, bridging the gap, 161
   machinations, 7
accountability

   in Caribbean churches, 145

   mutual, clergy and laity, 105
activism, 10
Africa, 37
Afro-Asiatic, 43
Afro-Caribbean, 20, 139
allegorical interpretation
   Roman Catholic church's, 48, 103, 104, 106
ambiguity, 16, 40, 127, 128, 129, 130, 131, 132, 134
American television, 38
Amplified Version
   Bible, 32, 139
Andrew Hatch, 11, 13, 49
Anglican, 15, 30
anointing, 124
anomalies, 24, 83, 88, 141
anomalous, 24, 94
anti-intellectual, 37, 41, 56, 82
apocryphal, 23

Blackett, Harcourt, 49
Brahmanas, 115, 116
Brahmin, 16, 27, 114, 116
brainwashing, 40
Brazil, 50
British colonizers, 6
Bromiley, G.W., 40
Brow, Peter, 113, 114, 115, 116, 117, 153

C

Calvin, John, 106, 107, 109
Campbell, Howard, 20
Campbell, Wayne, 129
Canon (of scripture), 16, 61, 96
    as a catalyst for literalism, 100
    linguistic origins, 95
    literary, Jesus' attitude toward, 90
    Marcion's, 96
    as a standard of morality, 127
canonization of scripture
    and the emergence of the notion of heresy, 102
    arbitrariness of, 37
    leading to literalism, 100
Caribbean, 14, 45, 101
    and other third world youth's vulnerability, 37
    influence of North American evangelicals, 38
    Rastafarian Mini Summit, 1997, 20
    vulnerability to fundamentalism, 15
Caribbean Conference of Churches, 4, 49, 163
    conscientization project, 128
Caribbean Week, 50
catalyst, 7
Cerdo, 96
Chisholm, Clinton, 20
Christian, 11, 12, 13, 16, 18, 19, 20
    clerics' failure "energy", 12
    complacency, 11
    response to Islamic inspired terrorism, 10
    similarity with Rastafarian doctrine of scripture, 20
Christian's final authority, 52
Christianity
    anti-intellectualism in, 39

166

G

grace, 16, 67, 83, 132
gramma, 60, 65, 66, 150
graphe, 6, 27, 60
guilt, 32, 33, 53, 135

H

Harnack, Adolf von, 98
Harvey, David, 4, 163
hell, 28, 40, 117, 137, 143, 144
Heraclitus, 120, 121
heresy, 102
Hillary Beckles, 4
Hokmot, 125
Holder, John, 4, 10, 49
holistic, 21, 22, 25, 75, 157, 159, 160, 161, 165, 166
human phenomenon, 16, 42, 111, 118, 138
humanity
    Bible's use in crimes against, 27
    individuality essential part of, 93
    theocentric views about, 137

I

I and I, Rastafarian linguistic formulae, 139
idealism, 36, 50, 56
idealistic, 35, 88, 102
    appeal of fundamentalism, 37
    concept of inerrancy and infallibility, 47
    perception of the Bible, 21, 35, 48, 106
    Reformers' perception of the Bible, 104
Iesous (Jesus), 24, 147
ignorance, 19, 26, 34, 50, 119
immediate experience, 53, 134
incarnation, 140
income, 24, 50
index, 10
India, 114, 115
individual, 93, 153
faith, 107, 153
    psychological effect of disillusionment on, 37
individual autonomy

170

Interschool Christian Fellowship, 155
intuitionism, 126, 131
Islamic, 10, 11, 27
Israel, 111, 112, 117, 153

J

Jehovah's Witnesses, 46
Jesus of Nazareth, 61, 118, 140
Jesus Seminar, 56
Jesus of Nazareth, 52
Jewish, 27, 43
    ambivalence about the Written Law, 79
    and Christian canons of scripture, 61, 62
    Council of Jamnia, 151
    fundamentalists, 56
    techniques of oral transmission, 70
    understanding of "te gramma", 60
Jewish "canon, 100
Jewish assembly, called "synagogue of Satan", 89
Jewish Kabalah tradition, 115
Jewish legalism, 79
    Jesus' rejection of, 78
Jewish opponents of Christianity, 86
Jewish reformer, Jesus as, 98
Jewish scriptures, 48, 52, 90, 96, 97
    cited in 2 Timothy 3:16, 63
    the claim that they 'killeth', 66
    God's will, 76
    notion of being "God-breathed", 65
    value challenged by Jesus, 78
Jewish synagogue, Christians' expulsion from, 108
Jewish theology, 120
John's gospel, 78, 97, 120
Jones, Jim, 36, 39, 52, 129
Joshua, 24, 147
Judaism, 16, 22, 48, 60, 61, 67, 71, 76, 79, 80, 83, 86, 89, 96, 97, 100, 102, 104, 107, 108, 109, 118, 123, 124, 125, 150
Jung, Carl, 128
Justin Martyr, 70

K

Keats, John, 25

172

misinterpretation, 26
Montanists, 97, 98
Montanus, 97
Mooneyham, Stan, 144
morality, 13, 19, 43, 44, 45, 90, 122, 127, 129, 134
    private and public, 93
Mormons, 47, 100
Muslim Question, 11
myth, 14, 87

N

naive confidence, 41
Nazarenes, 151
Nazareth, 89, 91
Jesus of, 52, 116
New Covenant, 2, 15, 16, 21, 22, 42, 43, 44, 45, 52, 61, 62, 66, 71, 72, 74,
    77, 89, 90, 91, 92, 93, 97, 98, 99, 101, 102, 108, 109, 110, 111, 112, 113,
    114, 116, 117, 118, 119, 121, 123, 124, 125, 138, 139, 153
New Prophecy, 98
New Testament, 14, 21, 24, 33, 42, 43, 44, 45, 55, 61, 62, 67, 68, 72, 77, 88,
    97, 98, 99, 106, 112, 118, 148, 149, 156
Noel Titus, 4

O

objectivity, 40, 100, 126
one-to-one witnessing, 31
oral teaching, 68, 71
oral tradition, 69

P

Packer J.I., 141
parables, 14, 84
Pastor David Durant, 18
Pastor Noel Goddard, 18
pedagogical pedophilia, 12
Pentecostal, 23, 24, 31, 50, 92, 164
Pentecostals, 23, 30, 42, 43, 46, 92, 93, 110
People's Cathedral, 164
perfectionist, 17, 47, 76, 131
perfectionist dilemma, 56
perfectionistic, 88
Persia, 116, 154
personal religion, 117

personal victory, 25
personally experienced word of God, 77
Peter (apostle) 41
    epistle, 59, 73, 80, 140
Pharisees, 86
Philo, 60, 120, 121
Pidgeon, Michael, 27, 154
plain meaning, 22, 24, 41, 42, 59, 69, 105, 129, 135
    fundamentalist disagreement on, 54
    obscurity of, 54
politicians, 7
Pope, 8, 47, 50, 104
Pope John Paul II, 50
post fundamentalist syndrome, 37
power, 103, 114, 116
    absolute, 104, 106, 109
    vacuum, 99
prejudice, 19, 26, 28, 71, 81, 100, 137, 171
preoccupation, 38, 143
    Christians', with scripture, 100
    emergent Christians' (former Jews') with scripture, 108
    Jesus', with scripture, 79
    Jews', with scripture, 62
    with scripture, 76
    with tradition, 69
presupposition, 49, 87, 104
priestcraft, 22, 94, 113, 114, 115, 116, 132, 137, 153
profitability
    Bible's, 130, 137
    of scripture, 63, 67
prophecies, 73
Protestants, 47, 105, 106

Q

quintessence of spirituality, 13

R

Ras Iral Jabari Talma, 20
Rastafarian, 19, 20, 52, 139, 161
    Mini-summit, 1997, 20

syneidesis, 121, 122, 123, 126, 127, 133

T

Tafari, Ikal, 20
terror of the Bible, 19, 21, 28, 34, 45, 46, 48, 51, 57, 75, 76, 80, 82, 89, 90, 94, 95, 96, 102, 103, 106, 107, 108, 109, 114, 152
Tertullian, 62, 72, 97, 98
testimony, 123, 126, 133
theology
    anthropocentric, 136
    emerging Protestant, 106
    Jewish, 120
    systematic, 49
    systematic or dogmatic, 53
Third World (reggae band), 20
tithe, 24, 105
Torah Code, 56
tradition, 15, 48, 51, 54, 69, 70, 71, 73, 79, 80, 90, 115
traditional Churches, 41
transliteration, 24, 147

U

uniqueness of Christianity, 113, 119, 124, 132
Universal Church of the Kingdom of God, 50
University of the West Indies, 4, 7, 126

V

Vatican, 7
Vatican library, 81

W

Wesleyans, 46
western society, 31
Williams, Holmes, 18
Williams, Rowan, Anglican Bishop, 11
World Conference Against Racism, 170

Y

Youth With a Mission, 142

Z

zeal, 53, 105
Zoroaster (Zarathushtra), 116, 117

Lightning Source UK Ltd.
Milton Keynes UK
UKOW02f1019241016

285992UK00001B/57/P